The Real World of
finance

The Real World of
finance

12 Lessons for the
21st Century

JAMES SAGNER

John Wiley & Sons

658,15

$12 r

ISBN: 0-471-20997-X

Printed in the United States of America

10 9 8 7 6 5 4 3 2 1

For Stephen, Amy, and Robert-Paul

contents

acknowledgments

This book developed from my teaching and consulting experiences going back three decades. Working with Fortune 500 clients, I have been constantly amazed that finance is almost an afterthought in the everyday world of business—except, of course, for such financial services companies as banks and securities firms.

Business today focuses on three priorities:

- Sell product.
- Install and maintain information systems to tell management where it is and where it may be going.
- Make profits.

Finance is expected to provide permanent capital for investments and to manage working capital to meet ongoing requirements. But it is not supposed to get involved in the management of the business. If you don't believe this, visit the financial function of a company and ask if any senior manager has ever gone on a sales call, toured the manufacturing floor, or talked to an unhappy customer.

When I teach finance courses, I often explain that although the book says "X," the real world operates in a "Y" mode. Students without significant work experience don't understand this. Those who are in corporate positions, usually part-time MBA students, immediately agree. And the question always is: Why doesn't someone write a book based on reality?

My gratitude goes to all of the students and managers I have encountered over the years. They have educated me to a far greater extent than I have ever taught or advised them. I specifically acknowledge the following:

- My first finance course at Washington & Lee University, taught by Professor Leland McCloud, using the text *The Financial Policy of Corporations,* 5th ed., by Arthur S. Dewing (New York: Ronald Press Co., 1953).
- Rosemary Loffredo, assistant treasurer of International Paper, who was my copresenter of an early version of this topic at the annual Association of Financial Professionals in Chicago on October 15, 2001.
- Timothy Burgard, my Wiley editor, who shepherded this book through to publication.

Grateful acknowledgment is extended for the permission granted by the following publications for the use of lesson 12 material that originally appeared in somewhat different formats.

- To the Association of Financial Professionals for "Roles of the CFO in the 21st Century," *AFP Exchange,* September/October 2001, Volume 21, Number 5. ©2001, pages 70–78; all rights reserved.
- To Financial Executives International for "Today's Treasury Function," *Financial Executive,* January/February 2002, Volume 18, Number 1. ©2002, pages 55–56; all rights reserved.

For any and all errors, I am entirely responsible.

He who can, does. He who cannot, teaches.

—George Bernard Shaw,
Man and Superman

What did they teach in your MBA or undergraduate finance courses? More important, was any of it based on real-life experience, or did a Ph.D. draw charts and write arcane formulae on the blackboard? And can you still remember what NPV, IRR, ECR, LIBOR, bp, Reg Q, and ACH mean? And should you care?

NEW ECONOMY CHIEF FINANCIAL OFFICER

Financial managers in the next decade will face complexities in several areas not even discussed in the classroom. Examples of these changing issues include company profitability, audit and control, the external focus of the chief financial officer (CFO), financial responsibilities outside of the finance organization, commercial and investment banker relationships, and the role of the rating agencies. This book discusses these challenges in the context of the twenty-first century "new" economy from the perspectives of the working CFO rather than the textbook CFO.

Why the new economy? And what's wrong with the old economy? The old economy has been driven by industrial production, resulting in systems of manufacturing and mass marketing. The CFO's job in the old economy was relatively simple, because of certain consistencies in the way business has been conducted:

- *A continuation of similar sales and expense factors.* Even in periods of significant inflation, we assume that we can forecast and control our income statement results and can construct a balance sheet that supports our business requirements.

- *Insignificance of the time value of money.* We assume away short-term interest costs and do not adjust for long production cycles and delayed payment terms.
- *Consistent patterns of customer and vendor relationships.* We have done business with Joe or Jane for 15 years, and the results are predictable and reliable. Sure, there was a quality problem eight years ago, and three years ago delivery schedules were missed by several weeks. But these vendors are our friends.

The new economy—focusing on finance, information, and people—is destroying these constants and forcing CFOs and other senior managers to completely reexamine the way they do business.[1] E-commerce is globalizing commerce, and you will be buying from or selling to companies in all parts of the globe. Business is changing—and the CFO had better adjust to this new world.

FINANCIAL FABLES AND MISINFORMATION

Here are a dozen lessons taught to every finance student:

1. Profits and returns on equity (ROEs) are the number-one goal of business.
2. Working capital is a store of value and should be managed to attain a high current asset–to–current liability relationship.
3. Finance is a specialized staff responsibility.
4. Companies should "own" critical finance functions.
5. Capital markets allocate funds to creditworthy businesses at reasonable cost for purposes of funding operating activities and strategic investments.
6. Banks offer a range of noncredit services to corporate borrowers at reasonable prices as a marketing component to their lending activities.
7. Capital budgeting procedures support strategic planning.

8. Rating agencies provide objective evaluations to lenders, creditors, and investors of the financial position of the corporation under review.
9. Investment bankers provide professional advice to companies on the structure of their balance sheets, how to raise debt and equity, and similar matters.
10. Auditors provide control and prevent fraud.
11. Risk management involves individual functions of insurance, financial engineering, and safety programs.
12. CFOs minimize capital costs and maximize returns.

Not one of these axioms is true although they all certainly sound logical. This book discusses the mythology of each of these financial "truths" and reviews current practices based on consulting experiences with close to 50 percent of the companies in the Fortune 500.

WHY GETTING IT RIGHT MATTERS

Why does it matter if these financial truths aren't completely valid? After all, the disciplines of business and economics are far from exact sciences. We're never quite certain if the Federal Reserve's action in lowering or raising interest rates will affect economic activity in the way that's expected, or if a new marketing or advertising program will sell the latest model car, toothpaste, or beer.

The reason it matters is that we structure our business lives to meet the expectations of debtholders, investors, analysts, and boards of directors with regard to certain truths. If they are not valid, then the most basic processes of finance—earnings reports, capital strategies, rating agencies and investment bankers presentations, risk management programs—are flawed and quite possibly misleading to us and to others. And misleading or inappropriate actions lead to wrong assumptions, decisions, and allocations of scarce (and sometimes irreplaceable) capital as well as flawed business schemes, markets, products, and technologies.

The use of invalid financial concepts is a significant problem in the current environment of evolving business complexity. Finance is experiencing rapid change through the development of sophisticated management tools that repackage traditional instruments or risks into their component elements. This repackaging allows the transfer or sale of each portion of the risk or instrument to investors, increasing overall economic efficiency.

For example, many risks can now be managed through hedging or the use of derivatives. Mortgages are packaged into collateralized mortgage obligations (CMOs) and sold as Ginnie Maes, Fannie Maes, and other investment instruments. We clearly do not want a sophisticated discipline potentially involving billions of dollars to be founded on a flawed set of principles.

DO BAD FINANCIAL DECISIONS OCCUR?

Financial misinformation, myths, and myopia interfere with the development of effective decision making and the optimal allocation of capital. We depend on a body of knowledge to allow us to conduct our business activities. Yet half-truths pervade business practice, often causing significant damage to companies and entire industries.

Do bad decisions occur? A listing of flawed business decisions would fill a library.[2] The next section reviews the Sunbeam situation, the dot.com bubble, the telecommunications industry, and the Enron debacle.

Sunbeam Corporation

In the fall of 1996, the new chairman of Sunbeam Corporation, Al Dunlap, announced that he would eliminate 6,000 jobs (half of the company's workforce), close 16 of 26 factories, sell off divisions making products inconsistent with the core product line, and annually launch 30 new products and save $225 million. Dunlap had formerly led Scott Paper (now part of Kimberly Clark), where he eliminated about one-third of that company's workforce.

Sunbeam's Plans.   The plan at Sunbeam was to build up the international small appliance business based on the Sunbeam and Oster brand names. Some analysts were enthusiastic about the plan; others were skeptical because of the impact of the staff cuts on product introductions and other strategic initiatives. Sunbeam's balance sheet listed $200 million in debt.

To raise cash in the fall of 1997, Sunbeam sold $60 million in accounts receivable and initiated an early-buy program for gas grills, allowing retailers to "purchase" grills in November and December of 1997 but not pay until mid-1998. Once the retailers were loaded up with grills, Sunbeam started a second sales program. A bill-and-hold plan permitted customers to buy and store their unpaid merchandise in Sunbeam's facilities. The two sales arrangements accounted for a major portion of the revenue gains in 1997 but were in fact future sales booked now.

On April 3, 1998, Sunbeam shocked the stock market when it announced that it would post a first-quarter 1998 loss on lower sales. After one-time charges of $0.43 per share, the loss per share was $0.52 in the first quarter of 1998 compared with earnings per share of $0.08 in the same 1997 period. Domestic sales, representing 74 percent of total revenues in the quarter, declined 15.4 percent from the 1997 quarter due to lower price realization and unit volume declines.

Sunbeam Results.   As the result of Sunbeam's alleged misleading actions, a series of class-action lawsuits were filed on behalf of all persons who purchased the common stock of Sunbeam Corporation in the 1997–1998 period. The complaints charged Sunbeam with issuing a series of materially false and misleading statements regarding sales and earnings during that period. The alleged misstatements and omissions were made in an effort to convince the investing public of Sunbeam's continuing double-digit quarterly sales and earnings growth.

By 1998, the balance sheet showed $2 billion in debt, a negative cash flow, and a net worth of a negative $600 million. In June, Sunbeam Corp.'s board of directors terminated Dunlap, citing poor financial results, marking the end of his two-year stint at the company. The scorecard was 12,000 employees eliminated, huge losses, and a demoralized company. "We lost confidence in [Dunlap's] ability to move the company forward," said one of the directors.

The focus on short-term earnings rather than thoughtful longer-term strategies forced extreme cost cutting, demoralized employees, angry retailers, and manipulated sales results to meet market expectations. Eventually, legal action was taken by stockholders, and in 2001, the Securities and Exchange Commission (SEC) sued Dunlap and four other former senior managers, charging fraud.

Internet Debacle

Many investors and lenders wonder what they were thinking—and what the CFOs who supposedly should have known better were thinking—in buying, hyping, and managing Internet stocks on the basis of new economy business models. Instead of ROEs and cash, we heard concepts like "eyeballs" and "hit metrics" that supposedly measured customer interest. However, logging on to a website does not book any sales or pay any bills.

The problem with many dot.com companies was that they had no viable business model that had been field-tested in actual market conditions. In fact, numerous strategies actually were contradictory to long-established business practices. We note three of these in the next sections.[3]

Illogical Plans.   Supermarkets have existed for decades on margins less than 2 percent of sales. Profits depend on bulk purchasing, low labor costs (except for such specialized workers as butchers and bakers), low site costs, and consumer participation in the buying activity. When online groceries promised competitive pricing and free delivery, they failed to appreciate the cost incurred in order picking and delivery now imposed on and accepted by the shopper. Consequently, most of these online companies (i.e., Webvan) *failed.*[4]

Vague Plans. Several dot.coms have had vague business plans, spending tens of millions of dollars trying to find a viable strategy. Often the original orientation was to develop a website that would be visited by a growing number of potential customers, who would develop a habit of returning to the site for guidance or ideas on such specific interests as women's issues, health questions, or investment advice. The dot.coms would make most of their revenue from advertising on the site, and some would generate fees from related ancillary services. Unfortunately, most of these companies never attracted enough "eyeballs" or advertisers and have not survived (i.e., drkoop.com).

Naive Plans. All businesses (except those with protected monopolies) must constantly monitor what the competition may be planning, particularly in response to initiatives that threaten their survival. Rival companies may not care if you introduce a new color or a new shape to your widgets. They will care if you develop a technology that eliminates the need for widgets.

The dot.com industry generally paid little attention to the appearance of companies that directly competed for the same customers using similar screen appearances, pricing, and marketing appeals. The ease of Internet browsing makes competitive shopping an inherent problem, and various studies show limited customer loyalty to specific sites. Furthermore, established retailers (i.e., Wal-Mart) with nearly unlimited capital have developed their own e-commerce activities to retain loyal customers.

A Dot.Com Success. There have been a few near successes in terms of control of a specific market, satisfactory service, and customer loyalty, with the most notable being Amazon.com. However, even with nearly 20 million customers, the company has yet to make a profit, and it reported a loss of $1.4 billion in the most recent 12-month reporting period, the fiscal year ending December 2000. Amazon's accumulated net worth is a negative $2.3 billion, and with books and other merchandise offered at a 20 to 40 percent discount from retail, there continues to be doubt that the company can ever make a fair return. Meanwhile, cash reserves are quickly running down at many dot.coms, and some four or five dozen may have less than one year of funds remaining.[5]

Telecommunications Industry

Telecommunications was a glamour industry in the last years of the twentieth century, due to global deregulation,[6] new products and services, and excitement in the financial markets. However, the industry was actually in some disorder, due to competing technologies (i.e., wireline or wireless, narrowband or broadband), many new companies, unrealistic borrowing commitments and equity investments in capital assets, and cutthroat price competition.

In just the 1996 to 1999 period, total spending exceeded $350 billion, with $85 billion in debt and $25 billion in equity raised to construct communications networks.[7] Stock prices of telecom service companies and their equipment suppliers plummeted as investors lost faith in the ability of the established companies (e.g., AT&T, certain of the Baby Bells) to compete, while realizing the uncertainty of these high fixed-investment business plans. Debt exceeds $700 billion in the United States and Europe, and a significant portion is likely to go into default.

Telecom Results. The CFOs of the various telecom companies made three mistakes in this potential financial debacle:

1. *Dependence on debt.* CFOs permitted telecom companies to become addicted to debt capital, erroneously believing that the lower explicit cost of debt justified huge infusions of bond financing. One example is AT&T, which increased its long-term liability position from $7 billion in 1998 to $57 billion just two years later.

2. *Reliance on investment bankers.* CFOs relied on investment bankers to provide guidance on financing and on bondholder and shareholder expectations. While the markets absorbed the securities (at increasingly higher costs), it is not clear that totally objective and accurate advice was provided. Investment bankers receive substantial fee income when deals are done; feeding an addiction may not be good ethics, but it's good business, at least in the short-term when the brokers' bonuses are paid.

3. *Absence of viable contingency plans.* Capital spending soared but revenue growth was only moderate during this period. When returns on equity begin to decline—the industry's returns fell from about 14 percent in 1996 to about 6 percent by 2000—the CFO must quickly implement appropriate contingency plans. These may involve reductions in capital plans, companywide reviews of expenses, and other actions. AT&T apparently did none of these things, and instead overpaid for acquisitions and did not adequately respond when revenue growth projections did not materialize.

The inevitable result will be consolidation, failure, and reorganization until the economics of the industry rationalizes.[8] Meanwhile, more nimble competitors, who are unencumbered by investments in fixed assets, offer such new technology to customers as fiber optics. Profit opportunities may reside in computer and Internet activity, and there is the possibility that data, priority delivery, and other features can produce value-added service and superior revenues.

THE ENRON DISASTER

Probably no situation in recent years illustrates more finance lessons than the Enron Corporation. Much of the story remains to be revealed in congressional hearings, court proceedings, and administrative reviews. However, we do know that the finance function became a key element in their business strategy, focusing on the trading of energy and such new commodities as broadband capacity and water services.

Enron created off-balance sheet partnerships to transfer marginal assets and liabilities resulting from bad global investment decisions in water and power distribution. These structures involved increasing complexity and risk, and had triggers that required the company to assume the partnerships' debts that included declines in the price of Enron stock and a downgrade of the credit rating to below investment grade.

Although the off-balance sheet deals were effectively guaranteed by the company, nearly every credit rating agency, analyst, and banker ignored the total potential liability to Enron. The rise in the common stock price (from $20 a share in late 1996 to $90 a share in mid-2000) lured investors, and these arrangements became a primary financing driver. However, as the stock price began to decline in sympathy with general market conditions, the company became unable to do new or to contain existing off-balance sheet ventures. By the fourth quarter of 2001, confusing financial disclosures disturbed investors and the financial community. The company's stock price effectively sunk to zero, creditors lined up to litigate, and the U.S. Department of Justice began considering criminal charges.

Ten of the twelve lessons in this book are reflected in the Enron story. Because of the limitations of the book, we are not discussing other considerations:

- The sad stories and lessons for the twenty thousand jobs and retirement plans put at risk by these actions

- The impact on the energy industry (Enron handled one-fifth of the energy transactions in the United States.)
- The company's dubious place in business history as the largest U.S. bankruptcy, involving $62 billion in assets (nearly double the second largest, Texaco, in 1987).

Lesson	Enron Outcome
1	Earnings were manipulated by shifting debt and assets to off-balance sheet partnerships. In addition, the company's accountants may have inaccurately recorded losses suffered by the company.
2	Management advocated new economy concepts, including the importance of intellectual capital and the drag of hard assets. However, cash flow must be carefully managed to finance current operations. By late 2001, Enron was burning cash at an estimated rate of $700 million a year.
3	In perhaps no other company in recent history did finance pervade the entire Enron culture. However, the company was engaging in trading operations that required a rigid structure of controls, including continuous marking-to-market of trading positions,[9] and the ability to quickly liquidate unprofitable holdings. These requirements were not adequately managed or understood by Enron's various businesses, and eventually contributed to the company's downfall.
5	Commercial banks ignored the basics of proper financial management, and continued to pump billions of dollars of loans into the company. J.P. Morgan Chase admits to $2.6 billion of exposure, and various analysts estimate that Citibank is owed $2 to $3 billion and Bank of New York some $2 billion.
7	Enron invested in numerous global businesses that eventually triggered the use of off-balance sheet partnerships, largely to hide their mediocre performance and avoid damage to the company. Among the worst of these investments were Wessex Water (England) and the Dabhol power plant (India).

Lesson	Enron Outcome
8	The rating agencies, despite having better access to company management than the average investor, failed to downgrade Enron's credit ratings until late 2001. As of this writing (early 2002), it was not clear if the raters did not understand Enron's complex financial engineering, were denied access to critical data, or were simply reluctant to downgrade the company's ratings.
9	Wall Street analysts and the investment banking community continued to promote Enron, even issuing "buy" recommendations as late as November 2001. It is suspected that the investment banking firms were concerned about preserving their existing or potential deals with Enron.
10	Internal and external auditors (both Arthur Andersen) ignored the secrecy, the lack of disclosure, and the complex structure of Enron's various financial arrangements. Andersen now claims that illegal acts may have occurred, and the SEC and other regulators are investigating. Andersen's own behavior in destroying audit papers has appalled business and political leaders.
11	Senior managers did not understand the cumulative effect of the company's various trading instruments and investments, did not run an effective "matched book" of assets and liabilities, and were trading commodities in unregulated and unsupervised markets.
12	The former CFO Andrew Fastow, following the lead of the former CEO Jeffrey Skilling, created this disaster, rather than managing capital costs and developing a viable financial structure. Their apparent goal was to support the Enron stock price. However, the CFO failed to establish reasonable controls or to establish an organization that could effectively monitor the company's financial activities.

IT'S BACK TO SCHOOL!

Each of these situations illustrates a lesson discussed in this book.

- *Sunbeam:* The mindless focus on profits (lesson 1)

- *The dot.coms:* The failure to construct logical business plans (lesson 5)
- *The telecom industry:* The bias of investment bankers (lesson 9)
- And of course *Enron:* The "poster-boy" for 10 of the 12 lessons

We could cite equally relevant real-life situations for each lesson using situations from the past few decades. However, the point is not to throw stones at the guilty—that could fill a shelf of books! Instead, we will try to develop a little common sense about the responsibilities and limitations of the CFO and the finance function.

Let's turn to the first lesson.

NOTES

1. For a more complete discussion of these issues, see James Sagner, *Financial and Process Metrics for the New Economy* (New York: AMA-COM Books, 2001), particularly chapters 1 and 2.

2. For interesting reviews of large company failures, see Robert F. Hartley, *Management Mistakes and Successes* (6th ed.) (New York: John Wiley & Sons, 1999); and Robert Sobel, *When Giants Stumble: Classic Business Blunders and How to Avoid Them* (Englewood Cliffs, NJ: Prentice-Hall, 1999).

3. A clever and insightful review of these foibles is the commentary by Maria Vickers, "Dot-Com Business Models from Mars," *BusinessWeek,* September 4, 2000, pp. 106–107.

4. For an interesting review of the Webvan situation, see Saul Hansell, "An Ambitious Internet Grocer Is Out of Both Cash and Ideas," *New York Times,* July 10, 2001, pp. A1, C10.

5. The Internet cash problem was discussed in a notable article by Jack Willoughby—"Burning Up," *Barron's,* March 20, 2000, pp. 29–32—which roughly coincided with the beginning of the dot.com selloff.

6. U.S. deregulation resulted from the Telecommunications Act of 1996, Public Law 104–104, allowing new market entrants to offer local, long distance, and global telephone service.

7. Stephanie N. Mehta, "Why Telecom Crashed," *Fortune Magazine,* November 27, 2000, pp. 125–129, at 127.

8. For one set of predictions on the industry's future, see "Telecom's Wake-Up Call," *BusinessWeek,* September 25, 2000, pp. 148–152.

9. Commodity and financial trading firms "mark-to-market" their own positions and those of investor clients to reflect the current value of holdings. This information is used to determine liquidity requirements and to request additional "margin" to support trading positions. "Margin" is a required cash or negotiable security deposit to secure a trading position, and is usually a small percentage of the total value of the holdings in an account. Margin requirements are established by the exchange on which a commodity is traded, but may be increased by individual firms. The Federal Reserve sets margin amounts for securities trades.

PART 1

Managing Financial Activities

The engine which drives Enterprise is
not Thrift, but Profit.

—John Maynard Keynes,
A Treatise on Money (1930)

LESSON 1

Profitability

What they taught in your MBA finance program:

Profits and ROE are the number-one goal of business.

What they should have taught:

Profits and ROE *are* the number-one goal of business. However, the widespread manipulation of earnings reports to satisfy stock market expectations and the imprecision of ledger costing systems make these measures largely meaningless. Instead, companies should manage from cash flow statement analysis.

DID SOMEONE SAY, LET'S KILL ALL THE ACCOUNTANTS?

Shakespeare's famous quote from *Henry the Sixth, Part II* was actually "The first thing we do, let's kill all the lawyers" (act IV, scene 2). And while that may not be a bad idea, the accounting profession could be considered for similar treatment. Accountants provide disinformation based on concepts that are centuries old, involving account codes and descriptions that have little relevance to twenty-first-century issues.

Profits are a seemingly straightforward concept as presented by most business school accounting professors. You take sales, subtract manufacturing expenses (cost of goods sold) and marketing and administrative expenses, and the outcome is net profits before income taxes. Subtract taxes and divide by the number of common shares outstanding, and you have earnings per share (EPS). Investors and stock analysts

17

multiply the annual EPS times a benchmark price-earnings ratio (P/E), and a "fair" stock price is calculated. If the result is
below the current market price, this may be the time to buy; if
it's above the current price, consider selling.

This sounds so simple that any reasonably intelligent person
should be able to do the calculation. However, the only concept
that we described that isn't open to manipulation is the number
of common shares outstanding. Everything else is subject to interpretation and occasionally even to fraud. And if earnings are
"managed"—to satisfy the investment community or for any
other reason—then business decisions that depend on accurate
financial statements are inevitably going to be wrong.

Why Profits Matter

By themselves, of course, profits or other dollar amounts (or,
for that matter, any denomination of currency) have no meaning. To say that we earned $1 million last month or last quar-
ter has information value only in the context of the investment
required to generate that profit. By common consent, the
measure in standard usage is the return on equity (ROE),
which represents the return on invested capital, stated as a percentage. A ROE of 12 percent can be compared to possible alternative investments and to returns generated by similar
companies in your industry.

As an illustration, the restaurant business earned an average
19.4 percent for the year 2000, while all public U.S. companies
reported ROEs of 15.8 percent.[1] But if your restaurant business
experienced a ROE of less than the industry average, you probably wouldn't care if you beat the other American companies.
To see the specific results reported by the restaurant group, examine Exhibit 1.1.

Results are obviously very dispersed from the average (or
statistical mean) ROE, with the established companies (i.e., Mc-
Donald's) being successful and other chains not doing as well.
However, managers of the underperformers have only a very
general idea from ROE or profits results that their returns are

EXHIBIT 1.1   Selected Financial Data for Restaurants

Company and Fiscal Year Reported	Sales ($ million)	Common Equity ($ million)	ROE (%)
Bob Evans Farms (April 30)[a]	$1,024	$462	11.3
Brinker Intl. (June 30)[a]	$2,474	$901	17.5
CBRL Group (July 31)[a]	$1,964	$846	5.9
CKE Restaurants (Jan. 31)[b]	$1,785	$350	Negative
Darden Restaurants (May 31)[a]	$4,021	$1,035	19.7
McDonald's (Dec. 31)[b]	$14,243	$9,204	21.0
Wendy's Intl. (Dec. 31)[b]	$2,237	$1,126	15.5
What A Hamburger![c]	$1,200	$600	13.5

[a]Fiscal year ending in 2001
[b]Fiscal year ending in 2000
[c]A fictional restaurant chain used in the discussion that follows

inadequate. Below-average returns may be traceable to any of various problems, such as competition, high food costs, changing consumer tastes, or other factors.

BUSINESS SEGMENT RETURN ON EQUITY

Despite the problems in using ROEs or other profit-based criteria, companies often calculate the ROE for each business segment or strategic business unit (SBU). This measure supposedly tells senior management which segments are accomplishing their goals and contributing to the company's overall success and which are underperforming and need attention. If we were managing Wendy's, we might use the industry ROE as a company goal and try to improve underperforming restaurants (or groups of restaurants) that were dragging the company's profit returns.

Strategic Business Unit Assignment of Equity Capital

The calculation of SBU ROE involves the assignment of total equity capital to each segment based on an allocation derived from some readily available standard measure, such as headcount or sales. Assume that the fictional What A Hamburger! chain had total sales of $1.2 billion, requiring $600 million of equity capital. If your SBU or group of restaurants had sales of $1.2 million, or 0.1 percent of the company total, you might receive a 0.1 percent allocation of equity, or $600,000. Your costs would drive an SBU profit, and that profit would be used to calculate your SBU ROE. Your SBU profit might be $75,000, so your SBU ROE would be 12.5 percent (derived from $75,000 divided by $600,000).

What A Hamburger's friendly founder and spokesperson, Claire Benjamin, may love your hamburgers, but she might not be as pleased with your 12.5 percent SBU ROE if the company's ROE were 13.5 percent and she's trying to get to 19.4 percent, the industry average. She may send in the engineers, cooks, and accountants, and tell you to hire cheaper help, negotiate harder with suppliers, work longer hours, market the stores through local events, arrange tie-in promotions with movie theaters, or turn up the thermostat to use less air conditioning. Will any of this work?

Variable and Fixed Costs

The income statement items under your direct control are your variable costs of doing business, such as wages and benefits, purchases of food and supplies, and, to some extent, your local sales costs. However, these variable costs—so called because they vary based on levels of sales—are not really that controllable, because certain standards of quality must be maintained.

You can't really order cheaper grades of meat, or wilted lettuce, or rotting tomatoes. Nor can you skimp much on the quality of cleaning supplies, on paper cups and plates, or on napkins. Besides, any savings on supplies may be fairly trivial. Labor costs are "sticky" in that they are subject to minimum wage requirements and, in some jurisdictions, union contracts.

The fixed costs in your restaurants are almost certainly beyond your control. You cannot easily move to a location at a lower rent, you don't set manager and supervisory salaries, and you have little oversight of such expenses as utilities, insurance, and equipment rental (or depreciation). And you will almost certainly receive an allocation of corporate overhead—for marketing, executive salaries (including Claire Benjamin's), and general administration—which you are powerless to manage.

Outcome of the Strategic Business Unit Return on Equity

There may be some "wiggle" room on certain costs, but probably not more than a few percentage points. If you aggressively pursue such expense reductions—and we'll assume that you do drive costs down 2.5 percent—your new SBU ROE will be 17.2 percent (calculated as $103,125 divided by $600,000) (see Exhibit 1.2). While you are still under the industry average, you would be doing much better than other What A Hamburger! restaurants or SBUs.

Is this a reasonable way to manage a business? The numerator of the SBU ROE is profits, which is derived from costs over which the SBU manager has little or no control. We have noted several of these expense categories, including the company's assignment of corporate overhead and certain local fixed costs. The denominator is a totally arbitrary assignment of equity, often based on sales or headcount.

Furthermore, what happens if we continually fail to attain our SBU ROE? Management may decide to close down our restaurants and accept the termination costs to cancel the lease and dismiss employees. However, the corporation's administrative costs don't go away; they simply get reassigned to remaining SBUs. Of course, that makes their struggle to meet the target SBU ROE that much more difficult, because the new assignment of corporate overhead to each surviving SBU inevitably increases with fewer

EXHIBIT 1.2   What A Hamburger! Pro Forma Profit Analysis

	Original	Pro Forma after 2.5% Cost Reduction
Sales	$1,200,000	$1,200,000
Costs	$1,125,000	$1,096,875[a]
Profits	$75,000	$103,125

[a]Costs ($1,125,000) reduced 2.5 percent ($28,125).

business segments. Before we discuss whether there is a better way, let's focus on inherent problems with ledger accounting.

MANAGED EARNINGS

Although GAAP (generally accepted accounting principles) is considered the foundation of financial reporting, significant latitude is permitted in the calculation of revenues, costs, and income. "Accrual accounting" is based on a sales date rather than the time that a cost is incurred, and a sale is recognized when an invoice is issued and not when cash is received. ("Cash accounting" focuses on the dates these events occur, but is used mostly by small businesses.)

Earnings Adjustments

The problem of assigning costs to sales is not a new problem, and was recognized and dissected as early as 1934 by Benjamin Graham and David Dodd. Renowned for investment commentary, these authors spent about one-quarter of their landmark text *Security Analysis* on understanding and recomputing earnings from published financial reports.[2] Their suggested adjustments involve:

- Restating nonrecurring income or expenses
- Eliminating any unjustified recognition of income
- Correcting any entries to net worth such as reserve accounts
- Analyzing methods of inventory costing and depreciation
- Adjusting earnings resulting from the operations of subsidiaries and affiliates
- Recalculating income taxes based on the preceding adjustments
- Including or excluding certain unrecorded assets and liabilities

Pro Forma Accounting

Financial results are now subject to various judgments regarding which sales and costs to include or exclude, whether to capitalize or expense certain outlays, and where specific activities will be reported. These procedures are generally referred to as pro forma accounting. Here are a few examples; you decide if the accountants made the appropriate choice.

- Have we made a sale if dealers accept delivery of merchandise for which payment isn't due for six months, and then only if the goods are sold to their retail customers? As noted in the prologue, Sunbeam used this technique to pump up its financial results in 1997.
- Is it a sale if invoices haven't even been printed? Some dot.com companies include "unbilled services" in their reported revenues, despite customers' right to terminate contracts at any time with no penalty. Covance and Parexel International used this strategy for fiscal year 2001.[3]
- Are earnings credible if critical costs are deferred because of sagging revenues? Eastman Kodak cut research and development in 1998 to boost earnings by over 30 percent.
- Is a company being deceptive by taking a large, current write-off to boost subsequent earnings? Cisco and DaimlerChrysler recently have used this technique to make future years' results appear significantly improved.
- Can we rely on profit reports that are smoothed by dipping into reserves? Reserve accounts are special balance sheet accounts established for possible future requirements of the business. High-tech companies often establish reserves to be used in future periods of slowing revenues.
- Do we have accurate data on the cost to produce sales if expenses are labeled as marketing costs rather than as cost of goods sold? Various Internet retailers have mislabeled certain expenses to improve gross margin results (defined as sales less the cost of goods sold).

Recession and Reported Earnings

The 2000–2001 recession has brought a new set of problems with reported earnings. In prosperous times, companies may attempt to hype current numbers. In a weak economy, a CFO is pressured to take his or her medicine now in the hopes of an early strong recovery and a surge in earnings. Of course, this type of manipulation depends on future positive economic results.

Current losses may be "loaded" by any of the following actions[4]:

- Reduce values of physical assets to lower future depreciation charges
- Increase estimates of bad debts to boost future earnings when remittances are received
- Account for restructuring charges now despite the uncertainty of actual costs
- Postpone the reporting of current-year sales to a future fiscal period to boost revenues

LEDGER ACCOUNTING PROBLEMS

The economic and accounting treatment of assets and expenses can be quite different. For example, we are not permitted to account for our most important resource—people—on the balance sheet, yet the economic value of human resources to high technology and various other businesses is unmistakable. The human capital issue is one of several problems in developing useful financial data. Some others are briefly noted.

- *Rules on depreciation.* Accounting rules determine depreciation and amortization periods rather than the useful life of the capital asset. For example, machinery may have a useful life of 10 years if properly maintained and operated for one shift, or four years if newer equipment replaces it, yet accounting depreciation may be eight years.
- *Aggregation.* Data often are lumped by ledger code without concern for the functioning of a business process. For example, banking fees are reported together rather than by the user strategic business unit (SBU) in the treasury department's cost center, and will not even be

properly identified if payment is by balance compensation. ("Balance compensation" involves the payment for bank services by balances left on deposit with the bank rather than by direct fee charges. A credit balance is translated to a fee equivalent by the application of a short-term interest rate, usually the prevailing 91-day U.S. Treasury bill rate.)

■ *Avoidable costs.* Accounting data may be difficult to evaluate because certain costs may not be avoidable. For example, space may be allocated to an activity at $25 per square foot. However, if there is no alternative use for that space, should the cost be included in a decision to outsource or eliminate the activity? Computer and telecommunication charges, administrative overhead, and other charges present similar difficulties.

Profits and Business Objectives

Despite the proliferation of accounting information systems and enterprise resource planning (ERP) systems, few complex businesses have hard data on profits by customers, products, and markets. ERP systems link company information through thousands of computerized data tables. Each table uses a series of decision toggles that direct the software to specific decision paths. Enterprise resource planning automates the various tasks required to complete essential business processes in a single package.

In the absence of credible data, SBU managers are forced to rely either on aggregated return numbers from accounting ledgers or on the sell-to-everybody strategy. Sell to everybody involves a shotgun approach, with the manager hoping that universal market coverage will result in an adequate number of profitable sales. Neither approach is particularly effective.

Management should focus its limited resources on carefully constructed business objectives that can yield significant and profitable results. An early step in our consulting engagements is to ask the Peter Drucker questions: Who is your customer? Why does he or she buy?[5] Companies may be able to answer that question in theory, yet our analysis of sales efforts shows wide deviation from stated business objectives. The smartest marketing organizations in the world have developed the data and the discipline for their salespeople to walk away from customers who fall outside of the defined market.

APPROACHES TO MEANINGFUL EARNINGS INFORMATION

We have seen that financial statements can be misleading, causing managers (and investors) to rely on results that fail to accurately reflect revenues, costs, and earnings. When the debt and equity markets accept these data and earnings actually were manipulated, shareholders and lenders may lose money. When managers use these data but reported financials are inaccurate, unfortunate business decisions may result.

For this discussion, the securities industry and the SEC can worry about the investment community; we'll concern ourselves about the management of your business. There are two approaches to the development of meaningful earnings information:

1. Regulatory agency action, to curb abuses by requiring adherence to GAAP standards
2. Changing to an alternative procedure, the cash flow statement

Regulatory Action

Arthur Levitt, the Securities and Exchange Commission chairman from 1993 to 2001, committed his agency to attacking financial statement "management," the manipulation of earnings by chief executive officers obsessed with making their earnings numbers. The current SEC chairman, Harvey Pitt, plans to promote an atmosphere that supports more reporting of company information including the value of intangible assets, although the form of this reporting remains to be resolved.

The major problems include restructuring charges, often resulting from closing a business operation; acquisition accounting, how a company handles various acquisition costs; "cookie-jar reserves," money set aside to smooth earnings in future periods; materiality, intentional management misstatements; and revenue recognition, booking sales before accounting rules allow the recognition of revenue.

Levitt's concern was based on numerous well-publicized frauds, including Mercury Finance, Leslie Fay, California Micro Devices, Kidder Peabody, Nine West, Livent, Cendant, and other companies. About half of the frauds related to the recognition of revenue, and several involved multiple techniques to manage reported earnings. Exhibit 1.3 describes what some of

EXHIBIT 1.3 Selected Recent Accounting Frauds

Company	Incident	Period
Leslie Fay	Misstated inventory and sales	early 1990s
California Micro Devices	Inflated and nonexistent sales resulting in charges of stock fraud	early 1990s
Waste Management	Overstated earnings	1992 to 1996 (settled in 2001)
W. R. Grace	Misstated earnings using cookie jar reserves	1993
Mercury Finance	Overstated earnings	1993–1996 (brought in 1997)
Kidder Peabody	Systematic intention to commit broker fraud	1994
Nine West	Revenue recognition	1995 (at time of acquisition of U.S. Shoe)
Underwriters Financial Group (UFG)	Overstated revenues and understated expenses	1995
Bankers Trust	Misappropriated security holders fund required to be escheated	mid-1990s
Livent	Shifting costs between theatrical productions	1998
Cendant	Accounting violations by predecessor CUC Intl.	1998
Rite Aid	Overstated earnings	1998–1999
Enron	Various accounting manipulations; see Introduction	Late 1990s–2001

these companies did. Pitt's approach would attack the long-standing dependency on quarterly earnings per share.

Enforcement agency concern with the manipulation of accounting results is primarily for investor protection. However, managers cannot operate their businesses if basic financial documents are partially fictional, particularly as some or all of the elements of a company's financial statements may be involved. If you can't depend on data on sales, or costs of sales, or net income, or your balance sheet accounts, how can you manage your business?

THE CASH FLOW STATEMENT

The financial statement that provides the most lucid presentation of a company's health does not report EPS, net worth, or ROE. Instead, it uses income and adjustments to income from the balance sheet in the presentation of the cash flow statement. This document is "cleaner" than the income statement because it allows insight into the quality of a company's earnings. While managers and investors are fairly knowledgeable about the income statement and balance sheet, often they are uninformed about the cash flow statement, the one report that is largely resistant to hype or creative accounting.

Components of Cash Flow

There are three major sections in a cash flow statement, although foreign exchange earnings effects also must be reported.

1. *Operating cash flows* show the ledger cash position; non-cash activities that impact income, such as depreciation; and changes in asset and liability accounts that affect cash, such as increases in receivables.
2. *Investing cash flows* indicate such capital activities as the acquisition or sale of equipment, or the company's realized gains or losses in its bond or stock holdings.
3. *Financing cash flows* reflect borrowing or repayment of debt, and stock sales or repurchases.

EXHIBIT 1.4   Significant Cash Flow Statement Adjustments[a]

Account	Possible Indication
Operating Activities	
Provision for uncollectibles	Problems with bad debts may indicate sales to poor credits
Accounts receivables	Slowing cash collections
Inventories	Falling cash balances
Accounts payable	Management is delaying payments to vendors
Cash from operations	Cash close to net income indicates quality earnings
Investing/Financing Activities	
Asset sales	Company needs to raise cash
Issuance of debt/common stock	Company needs to raise cash
Equipment or other capital investments	Decline could mean the company is preserving cash to manage earnings

[a]Assumes an increase in each account vs. sales.

Companies with prosperous operations will have positive operating cash and negative investing and financing cash. The latter reflects the paydown of borrowings from current operations and the internal financing of capital projects. Companies practicing creative accounting will have a difficult time with the cash flow statement, because cash inevitably reflects negative conditions in income and balance sheet accounts. For example, receivables that rise faster than sales, reflecting slowing business activity and delayed collections on booked sales, will result in a lower operating cash position. The information content of other significant adjustments to net income is described in Exhibit 1.4.

Two Restaurant Examples

We referred to the restaurant business earlier in the chapter, discussing the problems of the fictional What A Hamburger! Actual companies in the restaurant business provide a real-world look at applications of cash flow statement analysis. Of course, there is the ubiquitous McDonald's Corporation, with nearly 30,000 locations in 120 countries. McDonald's is too large and geographically dispersed to develop meaningful cash flow information for business segment use. Besides, McDonald's can afford a state-of-the-art ERP system!

For illustration purposes, we'll look briefly at two smaller, homogenous operations: Bob Evans Farms and CKE Restaurants. Significant cash flow statement entries for recent fiscal years are shown in Exhibit 1.5.

Bob Evans Farms operates about 450 restaurants in 20 states, serving homestyle meals with country hospitality. Bob Evans showed no particularly notable developments during the two years reported, although there was a significant increase in debt while stock was being retired. As the result, the debt-to-capital

EXHIBIT 1.5   Cash Flow Statements for Bob Evans Farms and CKE Restaurants

	Bob Evans Farms		CKE Restaurants	
	Year Ending April		Year Ending January	
Millions of dollars	*2000*	*1999*	*2001*	*2000*
Net income	$52.9	$57.6	($194.1)	($29.1)
Depreciation	$36.5	$35.4	$107.0	$104.4
Changes in working capital	$3.6	$10.9	($71.4)	($25.9)
Other adjustments	$1.0	$2.0	$186.8	$65.2
Total cash from operating activities	$93.9	$105.8	$28.3	$114.6
Capital expenditures	($96.9)	($68.5)	($74.7)	($263.6)
Other adjustments	$5.5	$33.8	$147.0	$52.4
Total cash from investing activities	($91.3)	($34.7)	$75.0	($216.2)
Dividends paid	($14.0)	($14.1)	($2.1)	($4.2)
Retirement of stock	($81.2)	($32.1)	$0.0	($9.0)
Issuance of debt	$73.9	($14.8)	($116.5)	$105.4
Total cash from financing activities	($21.3)	($61.0)	($123.0)	$91.8
Net change in cash	($18.7)	$10.1	($19.6)	($9.8)

ratio rose from 4.4 to 16.0 percent,[6] certainly within the average for the industry of 24.4 percent.[7]

We see that depreciation is well more than half of income, indicating that a significant portion of operating cash flow is from prior-year capital investments in structures and equipment. Bob Evans' ROE performance is driven by slow sales results and some unexpected increases in food costs and promotional expenses. The company continues to spend heavily on new locations and manages its financial and business affairs quite conservatively.

CKE Restaurants does business as Carl's Jr. and Hardee's in 3,500 locations, mostly in the United States. CKE Restaurants had a terrible fiscal year 2001, showing operating losses of nearly $200 million. Working capital deteriorated by about $45 million, which primarily reflected an increase in receivables.

However, cash from operating activities was positive, capital expenditures were reduced by $190 million, and the company is selling off stores to reduce debt and is taking other expense management and marketing actions to improve results. While accounting earnings were a disaster, the actions taken by management appear to reflect their recognition of the problems and possible solutions.

Single-product and many medium-size companies like Bob Evans and CKE can effectively use cash flow statement analysis to monitor financial statement activities and then direct appropriate responses to manage changing business conditions. Because the two companies are homogenous operations, their managements can quickly determine if problems are developing in certain asset, liability, or income statement categories and take remedial action as necessary. (See lesson 2.)

Larger, complex companies like McDonald's will have a more difficult time using cash flow analysis, as operations and financial activities are aggregated for the entire company. However, some large companies are developing reporting systems with financial ledgers organized by product or market sector, and can assign cash and other balance sheet accounts to specific SBUs for cash flow statement purposes.

CONCLUSIONS

Profits sound great in theory but are fairly meaningless when you are attempting to manage a business. Unless you have a very reliable financial reporting system, strategic decisions should not be based on SBU or operating division ledger profits. The continuing focus of the investment and banking communities on the most recent EPS is an unfortunate fact of life, and one that the regulators will be monitoring aggressively. In contrast, management's concern should be on long-term profitability using cash flow statement analysis as a guide.

NOTES

1. All data are from "Corporate Scoreboard," *Business Week*, February 26, 2001, pp. 55–79.
2. Benjamin Graham and David Dodd, *Security Analysis*, 5th ed. Sidney Cottle et al., eds. (New York: McGraw-Hill, 1988), chapters 10–20.
3. Reported in Elizabeth Macdonald, "Catch Me If You Can," *Forbes*, August 6, 2001, p. 58.
4. This section was suggested by David Henry, "Putting on a Grim New Face," *Business Week*, October 15, 2001, pp. 46–47.
5. See Peter Drucker, *The Practice of Management* (New York: Harper & Row, 1954), beginning at p. 54. This book is a classic discussion on how management *should* function.
6. Calculated as $25.8 million (debt) divided by $590.5 million (capital) for 1999, and $99.7 million (debt) divided by $624.4 million (capital) for 2000.
7. Calculated from 1999 data provided in the S&P Industry Survey for restaurants and dollar-weighted by operating revenues. Excludes companies with less than $250 million in annual sales and Tricon due to its debt-to-capital ratio of 130 percent.

Working Capital

What they taught in your MBA finance program:

> Working capital is a store of value and should be managed to attain a high current asset–to–current liability relationship.

What they should have taught:

> Working capital should be as close to zero as can reasonably be achieved. Current liabilities should be funded from operations and the ongoing liquidation of current assets, and all assets (including fixed assets) should make a positive, measurable contribution to the business.

IS WORKING CAPITAL IMPORTANT?

In lesson 1 we discussed the difficulties in using net income as a metric for the management of our business. Profits are undeniably essential regardless of whether we are old or new economy; just ask the former employees of, or investors in, dot.coms if the number of website visits or the time spent at a site mattered when it came time to pay the bills or meet a payroll. The problem with profitability is in the measurement, not the relevance.

Working capital, and indeed any significant ratio of business,[1] experiences the reverse situation: The problem is not in the measurement but in the relevance. First, the calculation: $WC = CA - CL$. Working capital (WC) is measured as the quantitative difference between current assets (CA) and current

33

liabilities (CL). A company with $50 million in CA and $30 million in CL has working capital of $20 million. In this situation, you theoretically have an ample cushion to meet debts that will be due within the coming year.

Old Economy Working Capital

Measurement of working capital using ratio analysis involves the current ratio (CA divided by CL) and the quick or acid-test ratio ([CA minus inventory] divided by CL). Good performance for these ratios traditionally was considered as well in excess of 1:1, with the higher the better. The greater the margin of current assets over current debt, the better the position of the company. For example, $4 million of assets compared to $2 million of liabilities is a current ratio of 2:1. If assets were $6 million, the current ratio would be 3:1, supposedly a preferable result.

Where did the idea originate that a large working capital position is favorable? The general concept of ratio analysis was first developed in the 1920s to assist creditors and lenders in evaluating a company, primarily to determine that debts would be repaid. Ratios were calculated for each industry for the median, first quartile (25th percentile), and third quartile (75th percentile), to show the "normal" range of experience. Results lying outside of the interquartile range were considered as unacceptable and worthy of corrective action. For example, a current ratio of less than 1.0 was often thought of as too low to be "safe."

The thinking that more is good was driven by the attitude of lenders that working capital constitutes a store of value to pay debts and bank credit lines. Financial analysts were trained to look at financial ratios and demand numbers that exceeded preset standards. In the past, this requirement often was used to force a company to borrow to put more cash on the balance sheet, which, incidentally, grew the bank's loan portfolio.

Modern Attitude toward Working Capital

The modern attitude among CFOs and lenders is that working capital is undesirable, in that it constitutes a restraint on financial performance. Assets that do not contribute to ROE are a drag on a business and may conceal stale inventory that may not be marketable and accounts receivables that may not be realized. The focus has evolved to the financing of CL from continuing activities and carrying only a minimum amount in idle CA.

The concept of working capital as a hindrance to financial performance is a complete change in attitude from the conventional wisdom of the old economy. However, working capital actually has never contributed to a company's profits or losses; instead, it just sits on the balance sheet awaiting disposition. No returns are generated directly by cash, inventories, or accounts receivable, and, in fact there is a significant implicit cost in carrying working capital. To help us understand this point, let's take a look at one of the restaurant chains that we referenced in lesson 1.

Wendy's International

Wendy's International, known for its friendly CEO and television spokesperson—the late Dave Thomas, had working capital of $65.6 million as of fiscal year-end 2000, comprised of $349.8 million in CA less $284.2 million in CL. A more appropriate industry comparison is the current ratio, which as a proportion does not require any adjustment for company size. Wendy's current ratio was 1.23 times ($349.8 million divided by $284.2 million). This compares to the average current ratio of the restaurant industry of 0.86.[2] Do these results indicate superior or inferior performance?

This question has two opposite answers depending on whether we are considering old economy or new economy finance. As we have noted, the old economy attitude was that the greater the current ratio—a generally accepted measure of working capital—the better. The philosophy of new economy companies is to minimize idle assets tied up in working capital. By this standard, Wendy's is doing worse than its industry and, in fact, has more than twice the working capital of such companies as McDonald's, Darden Restaurants, and Applebee's.

And we can see clear evidence of inferior performance by referring back to Exhibit 1.1, which showed that Wendy's ROE is well below its competitors.

Wendy's Excess Working Capital

Wendy's has $350 million in CA that are not putting any return onto its income statement. Of course, some of those assets (cash and equivalents of $210.8 million and receivables awaiting collection of $79.5 million) are used to pay its CL, comprised of payables ($126.5 million) and accrued expenses ($153.3 million). The remaining CA account is $40.3 million of inventory. Assuming that Wendy's must pay its bills within a reasonable time as they come due, the company still has a significant amount of surplus working capital and quite a lot of inventory, totaling more than $100 million!

Even assuming that a significant portion of inventory is necessary, there is possibly $50 to $75 million of "idle" working capital. The only way really to determine a more precise amount is to undertake a detailed study of vendor relationships and the logistics of moving food and supplies to the Wendy's restaurants. However, such an analysis may be worth the effort, as $50 to $75 million has an annual value of $6 to $9 million (assuming a 12 percent cost of capital or cost of funds).

DELL: A NEW ECONOMY COMPANY

This working capital philosophy has been implemented effectively by Dell Computer and several other new economy companies. Dell accepts ownership of components shortly before the start of manufacturing, driving raw materials inventory to minimal levels. Product is sold and a collection transaction is initiated concurrently, using credit card or electronic funds transfer, to eliminate most accounts receivable. The Dell CFO manages the operating working capital, or "cash conversion cycle," to attain a zero net time for days' sales inventory minus days' payables outstanding. Dell actually has attained a quarterly cash conversion cycle of *minus* eight days!

Aggressive Working Capital Management

Managing working capital to nearly eliminate CA and CL requires that cash not be expended to prepay for inventory or other operating costs, that vendors hold title to goods until delivery is requested, and that redundant expenses be eliminated where possible. A considerable inventory position is warehoused by cooperating vendors within minutes of a Dell factory and is requisitioned once a customer sale is booked. Since some suppliers are reluctant to do business with these requirements, Dell buys from fewer than 50 companies, down by 75 percent from a decade earlier.

Another innovation is the direct shipment of video displays to customers by the vendor based on an e-commerce instruction from Dell. This saves the cost of a second shipment, worth $30 per display.[3] As the result of these various actions, Dell's inventory turnover is an astonishing 63.8 times vs. 19.8 times for the industry, and its asset turnover is 2.50 vs. 1.43 for the industry.[4]

How does working capital affect Dell's financial statements? In the most recent reporting period (the fiscal year ending February 2, 2001), Dell's ROE was 37.2 percent, while the industry was earning 30.1 percent. And over the previous five-year period, the ROE of Dell was 63.1 percent vs. the industry's 32.2 percent. These results were accomplished despite lower gross margins (19.6 vs. 32.9 percent) and lower operating profits (8.1 vs. 9.7 percent) than the industry.

Old Economy Business Model

While our discussion of Dell may sound like public relations hype, a number of startling actions are occurring that defy conventional wisdom. The old economy model required holding assets on the balance sheet to create differentiated manufacturing, technology, and marketing processes. Few competitors could match an established company's blend of product offerings and distribution channels, and this special market position generated oligopolistic profits. Industries could continue in their protected status for years, confident that any disruptions could be fixed and that a challenge by an upstart could be met.

The vertically integrated twentieth-century manufacturing company often dominated an entire economic sector. Businesses like General Motors owned sources of raw materials, converted that inventory to finished goods, controlled distribution channels, and dealt with vendors only when special technology was required for a continuous flow of product (i.e., automobile and truck tires). Vendors, auto dealers, and even customers were their captives, and the accumulation of capital assets was critical to the perpetuation of this position.

New Economy Business Model

Dell and other new economy companies have introduced a different business model—one where results are based on minimum working capital, tight control over costs, low profits per transaction, very high sales turnover, and fewer owned assets. These outcomes require the application of several of the lessons discussed in this book, including finance's involvement in operations throughout the corporation (lesson 3), outsourcing (lesson 4), and capital budgeting (lesson 7).

An important element is the development of vendor/customer alliances or strategic relationships.

- Suppliers will become partners in managing working capital, because they will hold inventory until just prior to its use and will provide a level of quality that allows its immediate entry into a production process.
- Customers will be partners, as they will be expected to pay for goods and services at a time closer to the order date at a price that provides an acceptable profit.

If suppliers and customers cannot accept these conditions, then a hard choice must be made as to whether you will want them in your business model.

The new economy CFO focuses intensely on core competencies to determine the optimal processes to bring product or service to market at the lowest possible price. Often this means removing all but the most critical assets from the balance sheet, focusing on information technology to develop market and product intelligence, and using the most efficient technologies for internal and external communications (i.e., e-commerce). In summary, managers will prioritize *thinking*, not *producing*.

WHAT IS WORKING CAPITAL MANAGEMENT?

If the CFO attempts to drive working capital down to nearly zero, he or she must actively manage each asset and liability category. This may be new thinking since you went to business school, because the buildup of assets and the "inevitability" of liabilities allowed finance to focus on other, perhaps "sexier" matters: capital budgeting, foreign exchange, or derivatives. Today the discipline of working capital management is a growing field of financial practice, involving treasury managers, salespeople, accounts receivable and payable managers, order-entry and invoicing supervisors, and other specialists.

The importance of working capital can be seen by examining the balance sheets of businesses in new economy (and some old economy) industries. Continuing the Dell example, current assets constitute 70 percent of the company's entire asset base and about 65 percent of the assets of the industry (see Exhibit 2.1).

Lengthy texts have been written on each working capital account, which is obviously beyond the scope of this lesson. However, we note specific management actions for four working capital activities in the sections that follow. Each discussion refers to Dell Computer's management of its working capital position as compared to the computer industry.

Accounts Receivable

Accounts receivable convert to cash as customers pay based on established credit terms. Procedures to expedite the conversion of receivables to cash include factoring and receivables collateralization.

EXHIBIT 2.1 Balance Sheet Comparisons for Dell Computer and the
Computer Industry (SIC 3571)

	Dell (%)	Computer Industry (%)
Cash and short-term investments	40.5	13.3
Accounts receivable	21.5	29.1
Inventory	3.0	18.3
Other current assets	5.6	4.2
Total current assets	**70.6**	**64.9**
Investments	18.0	12.1
Fixed assets	7.4	16.9
Other long-term assets	3.9	6.1
Total assets	100.0	100.0
Accounts payable	31.9	15.8
Short-term debt	0.0	13.0
Other current liabilities	16.8	13.8
Total current liabilities	48.7	42.7
Long-term liabilities	9.4	10.9
Net worth	41.8	46.4
Total liabilities and net worth	100.0	100.0

Sources: Dell Computer data derived from its most recent financial statements, for fiscal year ending February 2, 2001; see *www.dell.com.* Industry data are from the Risk Management Association, *Annual Statement Studies,* Philadelphia, PA: *2000–2001,* p. 559.

Factoring. The credit and collection process, no matter how aggressive, inevitably results in some uncollectible amounts. When faced with the cost of the credit review process, bad debt expenses, and the cost of credit and collections, some businesses outsource their collection activities to a factor. Factors purchase or lend money on accounts receivable based on an evaluation of the creditworthiness of prospective customers of the business calculated as a discount from the sale amount, usually about 3 to 4 percent. That is, the factor will receive the entire sales amount, the selling company having received 96 to 97 percent at the time that the buyer was accepted by the factor.

Factor expertise has been confined to specific industries, typically those with many market participants. These include apparel, furniture, and general retailing, although recent users include start-up companies, companies in turn-around situations, and importer-exporters. Assuming the cost of factoring at 3.5 percent and average monthly receivables of $1 million, annual fees would be $420,000. Borrowing an equivalent amount at 10 percent would cost $100,000, in addition to which there would be some bank costs for the credit line. Although factoring costs about four times as much as a bank loan, many expenses are avoided, primarily maintenance of a credit and collection staff and the bad debt expenses resulting from uncollectible accounts.

Receivables Collateralization. In collateralization, a receivables package is offered as a security to investors. The critical element is a periodic, predictable flow of cash in payment of debts, such as credit cards, automobile loans, equipment leases, healthcare receivables, health club fees, and airline ticket receivables.

The market for public collateralizations is in the hundreds of billions of dollars, which has driven the required interest return to investors to become competitive with bank lending arrangements. Initial costs are higher than bank loans because the services of several professionals are required: attorneys; commercial and/or investment bankers; accountants; rating agencies (when ratings are required); and income servicers. However, the advantages of receivables collateralization are substantial—the transformation of receivables into cash.

Dell has significantly less working capital tied up in receivables than its competitors, primarily because retail customers pay by credit card and business customers by electronic funds transfer at the time of the order. Companies unable to avoid receivables and the subsequent collections activities should consider the use of factoring or collateralization in managing receivables.

Inventory

Just-in-time (JIT) requires that the specified materials be in the place of manufacture or assembly at the appropriate time to minimize excess inventory and to reduce wastage and expense.

JIT succeeds when there are a limited number of transactions; few "disturbances" due to unscheduled downtime, depending instead on periodic maintenance; the grouping of production processes to reduce the movement of work-in-process; and a significant focus on quality control (QC). QC minimizes downtime and the holding of buffer or safety stock to replace defective materials.

In traditional JIT, the company owns the inventory of components and parts, assuring access as the next production operation begins. New economy JIT places the materials at the manufacturing or assembly site, but title remains with the vendor until production begins. This relationship requires suppliers to optimize the stock of inventory, holding only those items that have been specified or are known to be required based on a statistical analysis of purchasing history. Both the provider and the user of materials are forced to develop a strong partnering attitude and minimize the adversarial stance often observed between purchasing counterparties.

Dell carries about one-sixth of the inventory of its competitors by requiring vendors to hold title and possession until just prior to the beginning of computer assembly. Businesses unable to accomplish such relationships with their suppliers should consider the implementation of JIT processes.

Accounts Payable

Various studies with consulting clients reveal inefficient payables management practice. Invoices presented for payment should be matched against purchase orders and receiving reports to determine that the vendor has met the terms and conditions of the order and that materials were received in good condition and in the correct amount. However, often in practice invoices are paid without ascertaining that all requirements have been met. In about one-third of the situations observed, no purchase order was ever issued nor was there a contract or other written agreement as to price or specifications.

Payables managers frequently allow payments to be issued well before the due date, particularly where no systematic diarying procedure has been established. A substantial number of companies have inadequate policies regarding appropriate purchasing and accounts payable practices. For example:

- Should the payment be released on the due date or some specified number of days after the due date?
- Are all cash discounts to be taken, or only those that provide a stipulated deduction? (We discuss this issue in lesson 3.)
- Can the requesting business unit choose the source, or does purchasing have the authority to select the vendor to maximize volume discounts?
- Has purchasing determined that approved vendors are legitimate businesses, with a suitable record of providing goods and services to the company and to the business community?
- Does the company support the use of procurement cards? Procurement (purchasing) cards greatly reduce buying costs, expedite the purchasing cycle, and empower individual managers to act quickly in the interest of accomplishing the work of their business units.

Dell has a high proportion of payables in its working capital position, regardless of the metric used. Balance sheet percentages show Dell's experience double that of the industry, and the ratio of the cost of sales-to-payables is 5.9 times while the industry average is 9.3 times.[5] Dell manages the liability portion of working capital by holding payables until the dates negotiated with vendors to maximize cash preservation. However, Dell claims to have excellent relationships with its vendors, who provide quality materials at the time required for delivery.

Cash and Short-term Investments

Cash and short-term investments are a residual of the operating cycle and, for this reason, are discussed at the end of the section on working capital management. As current law prohibits the payment of interest on corporate checking account balances, these assets are not literally held as cash. (Regulation Q issued by the Federal Reserve System prohibits the payment of interest on corporate checking accounts. However, currently there are proposals before Congress to phase out this restriction by 2005.)

Many companies use a bank product called a "sweep" to invest excess funds overnight. The sweep is a bank account in which all the funds above a specified figure are automatically transferred out of the account for investment overnight and then returned to the bank account next day.

Large corporations actively manage cash balances and invest in any of several overnight investment products to earn market interest rates; overnight investments often used by CFOs are listed in Exhibit 2.2. Companies that are borrowing against a line of credit use excess cash to repay debt, thereby avoiding interest expense.

Various services addressed in this book can assist a company in managing its cash position. For example, in lesson 4 we describe comprehensive receivables and payables; in lesson 10

EXHIBIT 2.2   Short-term Investments (in order of typical corporate investor preference)

Repurchase agreements (repo).   A holder of securities sells these securities to an investor with an agreement to repurchase them at a fixed price on a fixed date. The security "buyer" effectively lends the "seller" money for the period of the agreement. Most repos are overnight.

Commercial paper.   Issued by large corporate borrowers and backed by the creditworthiness of the issuer. An alternative mechanism for borrowing that is usually less costly and more flexible than bank loans.

U.S. Treasury bills.   The most liquid money market security, issued in maturities to one year, and backed by the full faith and credit of the U.S. government. Other forms of U.S. Treasury obligations include notes (with maturities of two to 10 years) and bonds (with maturities of 10 to 30 years).

Bankers' acceptances.   Irrevocable obligations of the issuing bank, created to finance international trade but often sold by their holders to generate liquidity for internal operations.

we discuss lockbox and the positive pay feature of controlled disbursement. A wide variety of cash management products are offered by banks and vendors, and they can assist in optimizing float (funds in the process of collection or disbursement), improving cash control and security, increasing access to information about the status of funds, and allowing the execution of cash transfers.[6]

Dell's cash and short-term investment position is three times that of its industry. In a sense this represents the result of Dell's working capital management efforts. It allows the company to respond quickly to market conditions:

- To positive changes in the business environment, such as the dot.com boom of the 1990s
- To adverse conditions, such as the economic downturn of the 2000–2001 period
- To investment opportunities, such as the acquisition of new technology or entry into new markets and products

Other companies in the computer industry currently are somewhat cash "squeezed" and have had to more aggressively reduce costs, including staffing; defer technology; or implement other crisis strategies.

CONCLUSIONS

The conventional view of working capital is that the higher the ratio or dollar amount the better, to provide a store of value to pay creditors and lenders. In the modern perspective, working capital is an undesirable drag on a company's performance, in that it is a mix of noncontributing assets and may hide inventory and accounts receivable problems. The questions the CFO should be asking are:

- How does working capital help my business?
- Beyond paying bills, how am I as a manager assisted by a large amount of working capital on my balance sheet?

NOTES

1. Dun & Bradstreet defines the 14 significant ratios of business in the categories of liquidity, measuring a company's ability to pay its debts; activity, determining operating efficiency; and profitability, evaluating the generation of earnings.

2. Calculated from 1999 data provided in the S&P Industry Survey for restaurants and dollar-weighted by operating revenues. Excludes companies with less than $250 million in annual sales and Tricon due to its debt-to-capital ratio of 130 percent.

3. See "Michael Dell: Whirlwind on the Web," *Business Week,* April 7, 1997, pp. 132–137.

4. Turnover ratios and other financial data are available at *www.multex.com.*

5. Dell: ($25.445 billion, cost of sales/$4.286 billion, payables), from its 2001 financial statement. Industry: Risk Management Association, *Annual Statement Studies,* Philadelphia, PA: *2000–2001,* p. 559.

6. For additional reference material on cash management products and services, see Association of Financial Professionals, *Essentials of Cash Management,* 7th ed. (Bethesda, MD: 2001), *www.afponline. org;* or James Sagner, *Cashflow Reengineering* (New York: AMACOM Books, 1997).

Financial Responsibilities Outside of Finance

What they taught in your MBA finance program:

Finance is a specialized staff responsibility.

What they should have taught:

Finance pervades every element of the corporate structure.
Financial management should be involved in all relevant
organizational activities.

THE "MYSTIQUE" OF FINANCE

Back in business school, you were taught that finance is a special subject with distinctive acronyms like IRR and IPO, buzzwords like "leveraged buyout" and "nondiversifiable risk," and
techniques like "time value of money" and the "capital asset
pricing model." In fact, this was all a form of class distinction,
to separate the accountants and the marketing students from
the supposedly "elite" finance people. Hogwash! Finance is no
more important than any other area of business.

By making finance special, or a distinct business function,
we ignore the reality that finance pervades nearly all areas of
the organization. The things that matter in the new economy
of the twenty-first century are people, information or "intellectual capital," and finance as measured by cash and access to

sources of capital. In fact, the old differentiation of line functions (i.e., sales and production) and staff functions (i.e., human resources and accounting) is pure baloney. Its original
use in managing the church and the military worked because
of their "command" orientation. The concept was somewhat
useful when applied to manufacturing companies at the end of
the nineteenth century.

How Will Finance Cope?

Financial skill sets must be extended to support the organization's strategic and operational needs. This broadening can be
accomplished through familiarity with the workings of the company, by participation in such basic activities as sales calls, tours
of manufacturing facilities, and discussions with employees in
a variety of line and staff positions. It is essential that financial
(and information technology) managers actually understand
what the numbers on their computer screens and bank statements mean rather than viewing the information as abstract
data without reference to the real world.

CFOs should encourage their staffs to a consultative attitude, seeking areas within the company for application of financial knowledge. Such functions could include business
forecasting, sales financing, systems design and make/buy decisions, accounts receivable and payable, and credit and collections. In fact, cash and information are critical elements,
because each step in the operation of a business involves decisions that impact both resources.

Cash Flow Time Line

Typical functions involved in business transactions are dis-
played graphically in the cash flow time line; see Exhibit 3.1.

The horizon axis represents time, and each activity along
the time line requires the commitment of days for completion.
Let's see how a typical transaction might occur for the sale of
product from inventory.

EXHIBIT 3.1 The Cash Flow Time Line

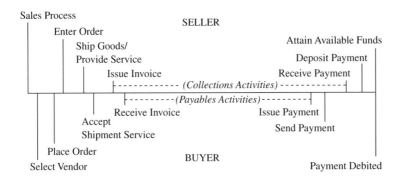

Raw materials and components purchase: July 15
Manufacture and assembly of product: August 1
Sale of product: September 1
Issue invoice: September 15
Payment due date: October 1
Actual payment date: November 1

The period from July 15 to November 1—three-and-a-half months—is a typical transaction cycle in business.

With the aggregated time often measured in weeks or months, each segment of time has a financial value or cost, as measured by the transaction dollars being managed times the cost of capital (or cost of funds) times the time period (measured as the percentage of a year). For example, assume our transaction is $100,000. If the company's cost of capital is 10 percent, there is nearly $3,000 in the cost of float, calculated as $100,000 \times 3.5/12 \times 10$ percent. And remember, this is just one cycle for one transaction!

Financial Discipline and Efficiency

We may manage the $3,000 using techniques described in lessons 1 and 2, but we cannot cleanse the business environment of float. However, many of the factors contributing to the cost *are* susceptible to review and improvement, although few managers realize that the improvement of their practices can lead to significant savings.

There are inefficiencies and inappropriate financial practices in many business functions not traditionally defined as finance. Finance is a discipline in organizations where managers, supervisors, and even clerks may have some "authority" without either the specific delegated responsibility or an understanding of important financial concepts. Such decisions often occur on the spur of the moment, in order to move a transaction along to its "successful" completion. However, success for the function—such as closing a sale—actually may be a mediocre result for the organization if the financial component of the deal is a nominal gain or a loss.

Exhibit 3.2 provides two instances of financial decision making for each of eight business functions. Specific examples of one practice from each organizational function are provided in the sections that follow.

COLLECTIONS FUNCTIONS

Three important collections functions are sales and marketing, billing, and credit and collections.

Sales and Marketing: Sales Financing

Is sales financing a marketing or a finance function? Industries as varied as automobiles and office equipment require sales financing assistance and analysis. Finance supports the development of credit sources for lending against the collateral resulting from the sale and can analyze credit terms and interest charges based on customer creditworthiness, asset life, typical payment experience in the industry, and other factors.

Chief financial officers can support the development of pricing models that consider repayment timing, expected transaction fees (i.e., late payment or origination fees), rebate costs

EXHIBIT 3.2 Financial Decision Making in Nonfinance Functions

Organizational Function	Action	Possible Outcome
Collection Functions		
Sales and marketing	Pricing concessions	Offering a percentage reduction for volume purchases
	Sales financing	Managing a program to assist in customer financing of products involving a large capital outlay
Billing	Invoice generation	Compiling the necessary data to prepare invoices for work performed
	Invoice review	Reviewing invoices for correctness, completeness, and compliance with contract and standard terms
Credit and collections	Credit policy	Extending credit to marginal customers
	Late payment scheduling	Allowing slow payers additional time to pay (beyond standard terms)
Enterprise Functions		
Information systems	Job runs with a financial element	Scheduling jobs at the convenience of Systems rather than to optimize cash flow
	New technology procurement	Deciding to acquire, build, or outsource upgrades to hardware, software, and telecommunications

(continues)

EXHIBIT 3.2 (*Continued*)

Organizational Function	Action	Possible Outcome
Disbursement Functions		
Purchasing	Materials and components purchase	Determining order quantity, price, and time of delivery
	Vendor selection	Ascertaining qualifications of vendors, including adherence to schedules
Payables	Invoice early payment	Paying prior to the due date (often day 30 after invoice receipt) or to the date established as the appropriate date (often day 45 after invoice receipt)
	Cash discounts	Determining whether to take cash discounts or pay on standard terms
Human resources	Payroll mechanisms	Making various payroll options available; e.g., checks, direct deposit of payroll, payroll ATM cards
	Direct deposit promotion	Requiring direct deposit as a condition of hiring; marketing direct deposit through a bank offer of free checking; etc.
Global business	International transactions	Arranging for the settlement of business activities in global markets
	Sovereign/country risk	Assisting in the evaluation of the business climate outside of the traditional economies

absorbed by the seller, and finance charges. As these types of transactions involve lending agreements, finance can assist the drafting of contracts, the disclosure of nominal and actual interest charges, recourse should loans fall into default status, provisions for the seizure and sale of collateral, and similar matters.

Marketing often wants to complete the transaction in order to take credit and commission-related income. Finance must consider the viability of each sales financing arrangement, protections for the selling company, the creditworthiness of the buyer and its customers, the economic environment, current and possible future actions by competitors, and the cost of the entire program. Alternatives should be reviewed, such as not supporting sales financing (and requiring the customer to arrange financing) or outsourcing the function to finance companies or financial institutions through full recourse, limited recourse, or no-risk arrangements. (Full-recourse sales financing involves lender advice and credit support with the selling company responsible for the loan; limited recourse limits the recourse, with each party assuming some risk; "no risk" places the responsibility for loan repayment on the lender.) Customer service concerns are integral to this decision and must be coordinated with any marketing initiatives.

Billing: Invoice Generation

Is invoice generation a billing or a finance function? Often a shared responsibility of sales, receivables (credit), and systems, your billing cycle may be managed based on access to the invoicing system without regard to the optimal timing of the printing/mailing process. There has been substantial research by credit card companies and other high-volume billing organizations that the optimal time for the customer to be invoiced is 25 days prior to the due date. However, many invoices are sent 10 to 15 days later than optimal, with the result that days sales outstanding (DSO) is longer than necessary.

Several other invoicing considerations may impact cash flow. Poor document design may confuse the customer, causing a misunderstanding of your billing instructions, due date, or "remit to" address. One of our client's monthly invoices cited four locations, including the remit to address, the company headquarters, the sales office, and the division office. No wonder so many payments were misdirected!

Mistakes also may result from multiple billing documents, such as invoices, statements (listing all transactions for a period of time, often the previous month or quarter), and past-due reminders. Rather than remit the outstanding amount, the customer may spend time researching each item to determine what has or has not been paid. Finance can help determine optimal billing patterns based on historical payment receipt patterns and can assist in the redesign of billing documents to minimize customer remittance delays and errors.

Credit and Collections: Credit Policy

Is credit policy a sales/marketing or a finance function? The establishment of credit policy involves four elements:

1. A measure of the ease or strictness in granting credit, depending on whether the objective is increasing sales or limiting bad debt experience. Granting credit too freely increases exposure to marginal risks, while being too restrictive may cause the loss of potentially profitable customers.

2. Limits on the aggregate amount of credit available to each customer. The determination of the credit limit is based on the experience with the customer and on his or her capacity to pay. The latter factor is measured by the buyer's absolute liquidity and by ratio analysis of relevant working capital accounts (discussed in lesson 2).

3. Repayment terms, including the timing of payments, the interest rate charged, and any cash discounts offered to induce early payment. Most businesses require monthly remittances from customers, although some expect payment as each invoice is tendered. Cash discounts may induce payment prior

to the due date or the normal time of customer payment, now averaging two weeks after presumed "net 30" terms.[1]

4. The administration of collection efforts for slow and no-pay accounts, including the arrangements for "workouts," the use of debt collection agencies, and, as a last resort, legal remedies. Most companies presume that some target percentage of debts will require additional efforts for collection and arrange for "pursuit" through various mechanisms.

Each of these policy elements has financial considerations:

- Easy/restrictive credit requires pro forma income analysis in considering marginal risks as credit customers.
- Aggregate credit decisions require analyses of customer liquidity positions.
- Repayment terms involve comparisons of effective returns from cash discounts vs. standard terms.
- Collection efforts require evaluation of the costs and benefits from each action as managed internally or outsourced.

Obviously, sales/marketing must work with finance to determine the appropriate credit policy in terms of the optimization of company profits.

ENTERPRISE FUNCTIONS

Two functions that span all time line activities are information systems and international business.

Information Systems: New Technology Procurement

Is new technology procurement an information systems or a finance function? Information decisions have been driven by information technology (IT), particularly concerning systems affecting the entire organization, even though many applications have substantial finance implications. The decade of the 1990s saw widespread acceptance of ERP systems, which include general ledger and such related systems as invoicing, receivables, payables, and treasury information. In many situations the CFO was instructed to support the decision on ERP or other software, on computer hardware, or on telecommunications facilities, regardless of cost, implementation effort, appropriateness, or expected returns on the investment.

With the cost of IT in the billions of dollars annually, the CFO must begin to exert influence on decisions for further investments. Finance must determine the value of these investments to the business, must assure the accomplishment of these goals, and must determine how better decisions will result. Too many technology decisions are made on faith rather than on a thoughtful analysis of the returns from the commitment of capital, time, and organizational cooperation.

Specific financial issues to consider in any IT decision include the following:

- Is the project's scope appropriate for the needs of the company?
- Does the project have a "champion" within the organization, or is it something that someone thought might be a good idea, perhaps an IT vendor?
- Are project staffing costs realistic?
- Can the project be outsourced to an application service provider? (ASPs are companies that sell access to software applications through central servers. We discuss ASPs in lesson 4 in conjunction with outsourcing financial functions.)

The resource of value in the twenty-first-century new economy organization will be information more than any physical asset, and it is essential to formalize the responsibility for protecting this asset and using it wisely and economically. In order to create the necessary defenses, a comprehensive plan should be constructed to identify your organization's information risks and to develop specific strategies to combat those risks (see lesson 10).

International Commerce: Investment and Operations Transactions

Is international commerce a senior management or a finance function? While many global deals are promoted by senior management, there are very significant financial considerations in striking and executing such transactions, including the credit of the vendor or customer and the country or sovereign risk.

The analysis of country or sovereign risk considers the possibility that transactions with international counterparties may be interrupted by the interference of the foreign government. Such disruptions may take the form of prohibitions or limitations on currency flows due to economic problems or for political reasons. There have been many recent examples of such outcomes, including currency restrictions in certain South American countries in the 1980s, in Mexico in the early 1990s, and in several Far Eastern countries in the late 1990s.

In the latter situation, several Asian nations, following Japan's lead, pursued economic practices contrary to those of free market nations. This included overinvesting in factories making products that could not be sold at a profit; oversaving, which dampened the extremely important economic stimulus of consumer spending; overregulating, which distorted the discipline provided by global competition; and (at least in Japan) the cultural tradition of *giri-ninjo,* or the retention of inefficient business practices because of feelings of commitment and empathy toward workers and the community.

In contrast, Western economies have encouraged investment but have never assumed that production surpluses could be managed through exporting and planned trade surpluses; have undersaved, according to many economists, certainly as reflected in the $5 trillion of outstanding U.S. debt; and have moved decisively toward deregulation.

These differences in country economic performance are significant considerations because of the promotion of international business through the World Trade Organization (WTO). The entry of China into the WTO, finalized in 1999, has reenergized

American companies in seeking opportunities in other countries with seemingly huge potential. U.S. companies want to be important participants in the Chinese economy and anticipate lower Chinese tariffs on U.S. retail and industrial goods and the elimination of the U.S. threat of trade sanctions.

Country risk exists when you do business in any sovereign nation, in that the rules and laws you depend on could change or be unenforceable in a dispute. China and other countries may appear attractive, but CFOs must be concerned with the country risk. Political, economic, or social instability could threaten investment in developing countries.

DISBURSEMENT FUNCTIONS

Three significant functions in the disbursement time line are purchasing, payables, and the management of payroll by human resources.

Purchasing: Materials and Components Procurement

Is materials and components procurement a purchasing or a finance function? Among the factors that should be reviewed are the determination of economic order quantity, price, opportunities for volume purchasing, and the timing of delivery of material prior to the beginning of manufacturing. These factors (defined in the section that follows) are the responsibility of purchasing following the instructions of manufacturing, although the combined effect of a buying decision has a significant financial impact.

Economic order quantity (EOQ) is a mathematical model used to calculate the optimal size of a materials or components purchase. It also is used in making production lot size decisions to minimize the costs of manufacturing and carrying inventory. "Price" refers to the anticipation of future price increases or decreases, calculated after taking all relevant cash discounts. "Volume discounts" refer to price concessions for quantity purchases as offered by vendors. "Timing of delivery" refers to the holding period of materials prior to the initiation of a production cycle.

The purchasing decision may fail to consider the cost of carrying inventory, the real value of volume discounts offered, or the potential loss from stale inventory. For example, one large manufacturing company frequently acquired materials and components far in advance of the start of the production cycle, resulting in excessive carrying costs and some unusable materials. The average holding period was 60 days, which reduced the realized gross margin by 1.50 percent, from 10 to 8.5 percent. The impact on the company's ROE was 2 percent, with the target ROE of 16 percent declining to 14 percent. The role of finance in this situation is to determine the EOQ, calculate the value and costs of volume discounts based on recent experience, and support decisions that optimize enterprise results.

Payables: Cash Discounts

Is taking a cash discount a finance or payables function? When cash discounts are offered, the general format is to express the terms as the percentage discount if paid within a specific number of days and the due date if no discount is taken. A typical example is "1/10, net 30," where 1 percent is the cash discount offered if payment is within 10 days, with the full amount due in 30 days. The annualized value of the discount to the buying company is calculated as the number of "full payment periods" in a year (18, calculated as $360 \div [30 - 10]$) times the discount (1 percent), or 18 percent.

Many managers would be relatively indifferent to taking this discount by early payment, as the relevant average cost of capital would be nearly that amount. A 2/10 discount *appears* more attractive, having an annualized value of 36 percent. However, recent ratio analysis of payment practices of American industry indicates that the average time to payment is about 45 days. This valuation method would show far less attractive results: 360 ÷ (45 − 10) times 1 percent = about a 10 percent value, with a 2/10 discount valued at about 20 percent.

There are several other financial considerations regarding cash discounts:

- *Late payers.* It is difficult to enforce terms should a customer pay late. For example, a payment mailed on day 11 or after on 2/10, net 30 terms is not entitled to the 2 percent discount, yet very few vendors will demand that the 2 percent discount be remitted as not having been properly earned.
- *Inadequate discounts.* Many companies have procedures requiring that all cash discounts be accepted, with expedited payments to legitimately earn the reduced invoice price. Suppose the discount is .5/10 or 1/10, net 30; it is likely that the resulting interest equivalents (10 and 5 percent, respectively) are below an acceptable threshold acceptance rate.
- *Who decides?* Fairly junior accounts payable clerks often make decisions on cash discounts, with no training on the value to the company of taking or forgoing the discount. Even the act of expediting a payment may shortcircuit normal controls in approving bills for payment: insisting on purchase orders, receiving reports, a thorough review of the invoice, signatures authorizing payment, and the like.
- *Failure to take discounts.* Should a pattern of taking the discount be established, any subsequent failure to continue that behavior may be considered as a sign of financial distress by the seller. Such a sign of "weakness" could affect the vendor-buyer relationship, in terms of the price and terms offered and the priority for vendor service.

Human Resources: Direct Deposit of Payroll

Is offering alternative compensation mechanisms a payroll and human resources or a finance function? Compensation traditionally has been managed by the payroll or the human resources department, with the mechanisms for pay based on the convenience of the company and the needs of the employee. The mechanism used most commonly in the past 50 years has been a check, often issued biweekly toward the end of the workweek. The banking system has developed an electronic alternative to the payroll check—called "direct deposit"—which is executed through an automated clearinghouse (ACH) transaction. (Electronic funds transfer mechanisms include clearings on a same-day basis (Fed wire) and next-day basis (ACH). ACH transactions are batch process, store and forward, with files sent to banks by initiating organizations and transmitted electronically to the receiving bank for credit to the vendor or other payee.)

The advantage of direct depositing is the elimination of paper, the completion of funds transfer the day following initiation, the elimination of outstanding checks and their reconciliation, and a much lower cost per item (some 10 cents versus as much as $5). Despite these benefits, direct deposit is the payroll mechanism for less than half of all U.S. employees, largely due to inadequate promotion by payroll and human resources.

After the process is introduced, companies typically fail to aggressively market its convenience, allowing a dual check/direct deposit system to continue. A promotional campaign could include tie-ins with local banks for free or low-cost employee checking; the location of an automated teller machine (ATM) on company premises; and the offering of other banking-type services (e.g., consumer and auto loans, credit cards, and discount brokerage).

Finance must become involved by arranging for local bank participation in the direct deposit program and by working with payroll and human resources to raise general understanding of the benefits to the company and its employees. Some organizations (primarily on the West Coast) have driven direct deposit of payroll to more than 90 percent of their employees and, in the process, have saved tens of thousands of dollars in banking charges.

CONCLUSIONS

Companies in the twenty-first century will organize themselves around different groupings than those of the twentieth century. The cash flow time line clearly shows the universality of finance, and thoughtful CFOs realize that what is important now includes finance along with information and people. These are the only resources that transcend all organizational activities and without which survival is impossible. Besides changing the focus of our form of organization, we have to accept the idea that all of us must become "expert" in the management of these resources. Ultimately, a failure may mean the demise of the business.

NOTES

1. The Credit Research Foundation (*www.crfonline.org*) reports average days sales outstanding experienced by U.S. businesses for the fourth-quarter 2000 at 43 days, vs. 45 days one year earlier.

Outsourcing

What they taught in your MBA finance program:

Companies should "own" critical finance functions.

What they should have taught:

Many businesses no longer consider finance as a core competency and realize that significant cost savings and other advantages may be gained by outsourcing selected financial functions.

FINANCE IN THE OLD ECONOMY

Finance once involved extensive professional and clerical staff to manage such activities as treasury, accounting, tax issues, international finance, merger and acquisition planning, financial policies, and budgeting. Remember, in the last lesson we explained that financial professionals consider themselves "special" or "elite." A financial function might have required a half-dozen managers who reported directly to the CFO. For large companies, there could be 100 or so in staff making accounting entries, calculating cash balances, ordering checkstock, reviewing loan documentation, and reconciling bank accounts.

When there were pressures to reduce costs, the initial focus usually involved reductions in headcount. This was later supplemented by the increased use of technology to perform such routine tasks as journal entries, repetitive money transfers, bank account reconciliations, and check signing. In addition, bank and vendor charges were scrutinized, and CFOs often were able to negotiate lower fees for information reporting; depository, concentration, and disbursement services; credit arrangements; accounting fees; and insurance premiums.

With financial deregulation and consolidation within the financial services industry (to be discussed in lessons 5 and 6), CFOs have begun to encounter fully priced services and credit rationing. Cost savings will no longer come from the negotiation of lower fees; instead, companies face significantly higher charges for bank and vendor services. As a result, internal improvements, outsourcing, and shared services must be considered in managing the finance function.

REENGINEERING THE FINANCE FUNCTION

Reengineering is the concept of redesigning an organization through internal changes and outsourcing in an effort to save costs and time, and to improve service. The application of this approach to finance was described in an earlier book.[1] It basically involves the determination of the costs of the current function and the calculation of possible savings through selected internal improvements. Other options include management of the function through a shared service center ("insourcing") or outsourcing through a bidding process to qualified banks and vendors.

Cost "Baseline"

The determination of current costs is a complex exercise, because many components are spread throughout various responsibilities (and budget or ledger accounts) in any organization. For example, collection processing can involve six different organizational units:

1. The mailroom
2. Accounting
3. Credit and collections

4. Treasury
5. Information systems
6. Customer service

As shown in Exhibit 4.1, relevant individual expenses are mailroom equipment, including mail openers and check reader-sorters; labor to process invoices, handle mail, apply cash received, research exceptions, and provide customer service; and space rental. Other collection activities include accounting systems; credit reviews and late collection activity; and banking fees and availability. "Availability" measures the number of days that elapse between the deposit of checks and their accessibility for investment or other use of the funds. A bank "availability schedule" lists drawee points or locations, specifying availability granted in business days.

Disbursement processing may require the participation of five business activities:

1. Purchasing
2. Receiving or warehousing
3. Accounts payable
4. Treasury
5. Information systems

Some 20 separate expense categories are involved in a complete disbursement activity. These include computer processing, various ancillary equipment (i.e., signing and bursting), and service contracts for the equipment. Labor expense involves the issuance of manual checks, check research, sorting and distributing, and the check control process; other costs such as check stock and envelopes, the warehousing of forms, and various banking fees.[2]

The difficulty in developing useful accounting information has led to attempts to improve the alignment of accounting and financial data. One such effort, activity-based costing (ABC), evaluates a company's functions to reconfigure the general ledger into logical business activities. In contrast, traditional accounting provides reporting on such general categories as wages, supplies, and cash.

EXHIBIT 4.1 Collection Baseline Cost Analysis

Annual Costs	Site A	Site B	Site C	Site D	Total
Equipment:					
Mail Opener					
Lease	$250	$300	$250	$300	$1,100
Reader/Sorter					
Lease	$2,000	$2,000	$2,000	$2,000	$8,000
Maintenance	$1,000	$1,000	$1,000	$1,000	$4,000
Other Equipment					
Lease	$100	$150	$200	$175	$625
Subtotal	$3,350	$3,450	$3,450	$3,475	$13,725
Labor[a]:					
Collections	8.00	7.00	6.50	5.75	27.25
Exceptions	5.00	6.00	5.00	5.00	21.00
Other	0.25	0.25	0.50	0.25	1.25
Management	1.00	1.50	0.75	0.75	4.00
Subtotal (FTE)	14.25	14.75	12.75	11.75	53.50
Subtotal	$31,350	$38,350	$29,325	$29,375	$128,400
Rent[b]:					
Per Employee	$15/SF	$22/SF	$18/SF	$14/SF	
Subtotal	$713	$1,082	$765	$548	$3,108
Total Costs	$35,413	$42,882	$33,540	$33,398	$145,233
Item Volume	74,000	60,000	75,000	65,000	274,000
Total Per Item	$0.479	$0.715	$0.447	$0.514	$0.530

[a]Labor shown as full-time equivalents (FTE).
[b]Rent is determined based on 40 square feet (SF) per employee.

Activity-based costing examines indirect charges to discern those factors that "drive" or cause these costs, such as the number of production batches, purchase orders, suppliers, or engineering changes. These drivers are the critical cost factors for many types of businesses, products, markets, or customers. This cost-driver assignment is essential to ABC, as standard cost accounting uses largely irrelevant aggregated measures, such as product count, worker hours, and square feet.[3]

Internal Improvements

Although the development of baseline costs is difficult, it is a necessary step to enable the consideration of alternative actions. However, once the relevant cost categories are identified, the impact of various internal improvements may be considered. Examples of possible finance efficiencies include consolidating processing sites, lockboxing, headcount reductions using part-time employees, improving availability granted by deposit banks, and computing on minicomputers or personal computers (PCs) rather than mainframe computers.

Internal improvements must be considered in steps and in the aggregate. "Step" analysis may show that full-time headcount can be reduced by 10 percent through changes in work assignments. To reduce headcount by 25 percent, it may be necessary to convert full-time positions to part-time work. A 50 percent headcount may be possible only through outsourcing, to be discussed in the next section. It is also important to evaluate the impact of one change on others. This consideration of the "aggregate" effect could substitute technology for headcount or might consolidate processing sites to reduce redundant costs. An example of this analysis is provided in Exhibit 4.2.

In the evaluation of possible internal improvements, it may be possible to justify "insourcing" (or shared services) on the basis of cost savings or customer service. This alternative involves creating centers within a company based on standardized processing routines. Once a common set of procedures is determined, often through an ERP common system, shared

EXHIBIT 4.2 Impact of Internal Improvements

Annual Costs	Current[a]	10%	17.5%	25%
Equipment:				
Mail Opener	$1,100	$1,100	$1,100	$1,100
Reader/Sorter	$12,000	$12,000	$12,000	$12,000
Other Equipment	$625	$625	$625	$625
Subtotal ($)	$13,725	$13,725	$13,725	$13,725
Labor[b]:				
Collections	27.25	24.53	22.48	20.44
Exceptions	21.00	18.90	17.33	15.75
Other	1.25	1.13	1.03	0.94
Management	4.00	3.60	3.30	3.00
Subtotal (FTE)	53.50	48.15	44.14	40.13
Subtotal ($)	$128,400	$115,560	$105,930	$96,300
Overhead:				
Subtotal ($)	$3,108	$3,108	$3,108	$3,108
Total Costs:	$145,233	$132,393	$122,763	$113,133
Item Volume[c]	274,000	265,000	265,000	265,000
Total Per Item:	$0.530	$0.500	$0.463	$0.427

[a]Current costs and notes are from Exhibit 4.1. There is no impact on equipment costs or rent from internal improvements.

[b]Labor costs reflect the following improvements:

10%: Some reassignment of personnel to reflect capacity studies and optimal use of staff.

15%: Substitution of some full-time staff by part-time employees.

20%: Significant realignment of staffing, including most full-time staff.

[c]Item volume: Slight decline in volumes due to elimination of some exception processing.

service centers can be established instead of each business performing its own processing. Functions usually managed in this manner include invoice processing, payroll, travel and entertainment reimbursement, payables, receivables, and the processing of collection and disbursement transactions.[4]

OUTSOURCING

Outsourcing involves the decision to transfer the responsibility for a noncore activity to a third-party provider. Traditional outsourcing activities by companies include legal, tax, and audit work; the preparation of payroll; and the servicing and maintenance of equipment. Recent financial initiatives have added invoicing, disbursements, receivables, travel and entertainment expense management, investment management, and selected accounting functions. In fact, if a competent vendor is located, nearly all of finance can be outsourced, perhaps excluding only the opening/closing of bank accounts and negotiating credit arrangements or the issuance of debt or equity.

Cost Analysis

In previous sections we considered various actions to develop internal improvements to a collection system. Exhibit 4.3 presents two outsourcing alternatives using combinations of lockboxing. (The lockbox, which we discuss in more detail in lessons 5 and 10, is the most widely used outsource service for accelerating the collection of remittances.) A vendor (usually a bank) receives mail at a specified post office box address, processes the remittances, and deposits checks received in the payee's bank account. A summary of the per-item costs shows the following:

Baseline (or current):	53.0 cents
Optimal internal cost:	42.7 cents
50 percent of the items lockboxed:	40.5 cents
All items lockboxed:	38.3 cents

EXHIBIT 4.3   Outsource Costs[a]

	Outsource to Lockbox	
Annual Costs	**50%**	**100%**
Equipment:	$6,863	$0
Labor:		
Collections	13.63	0.00
Exceptions	10.50	8.00
Other	0.63	0.15
Management	2.00	1.00
Subtotal (FTEs)	26.75	9.15
Subtotal ($)	$64,200	$21,960
Rent		
Subtotal ($)	$129	$44
Lockbox Charges		
Per item charge and maintenance	$0.325	$0.300
Subtotal	$43,063	$79,500
Total Costs	$107,392	$101,504
Item Volume		
Internally Processed	132,500	0
Lockboxed	132,500	265,000
Total Per Item	$0.405	$0.383

[a]See Exhibits 4.1 and 4.2 for notes.

While the outsourcing alternative is clearly the most cost-effective choice, potentially saving nearly $40,000 annually—265,000 items × (53 cents − 38.3 cents) = $38,955—the decision also would be based on various qualitative issues for each alternative. Such concerns might include service quality, error rates, disaster recovery capabilities, and other factors.

In conducting the analysis, we must be certain to include all relevant costs—not just the "run-rate costs"—when considering the outsourcing option. You can do this by getting a complete task description from the bank or vendor in its bid for the service, incorporating all steps, edits, reviews, and actions included in the bid. For example, the outsource vendor may impose an implementation charge during the initial setup, and/or a programming charge, and/or separate charges for high exception rates or special processing. In addition, there may be costs to abandon or sell equipment currently being used that has not been fully depreciated or costs to terminate or transfer current employees.

Qualitative Issues

Outsourcing has become a viable alternative to the internal "ownership" of financial functions—even critical functions—because it often fosters innovation by partnering with leading service providers. These providers often specialize in the particular service, and by spreading personnel and technology costs over a large client base, they are able to offer a superior product at a cost below the current baseline. Furthermore, outsourcing permits a company to concentrate on its core competency, which for most organizations does not include finance, a traditional "staff" function.

For example, a chemical company is in business to manufacture and distribute chemical products, not to collect and disburse funds, cut payroll checks, do accounting entries, or file tax returns. No particular value is gained by doing these activities, nor is any competitive advantage derived from issuing checks or maintaining the general ledger. As companies begin to accept this concept, they may give serious consideration to outsourcing. General Motors realized this in 1999 and outsourced its payroll, some invoicing, some receivables and payables processing, and travel and entertainment expenses.

The finance functions that can be readily outsourced usually are consolidated in a single or perhaps two locations, as is often found with treasury and payroll. If activities are decentralized, as may be the situation with accounting, outsourcers cannot easily accept multiple file transmissions or other input from the company. However, some organizations have used the outsourcing option to reengineer old, inefficient processes and then to decide whether to make internal changes or to contract with a vendor for the service.

OUTSOURCING FINANCIAL ACTIVITIES

Outsourcing can be a cost-effective alternative to internal processing for certain financial activities. Internal processing tends to be inefficient for many operations, often using processes that have not been examined critically in years. Service quality from outsourcing vendors is often higher than internal processing due to an authentic customer orientation and the need to provide a quality product. Two recent financial outsourcing offerings are discussed in the sections that follow.

Comprehensive Receivables

Collection receipts can be outsourced through a product generically known as "comprehensive receivables." The service permits all payment inflows—lockbox, straight deposits, and electronic funds transfers (ACH and Fedwire)—to be received. The items are deposited, and payments and remittance data are reassociated. The company sends a daily transmission of its receivables file to the bank in a standard format. When payments arrive, receivables are matched against each payment based on unique identifiers, such as account, order, and transaction.

The match of an identifier with an amount paid clears the receivable. If a match cannot be found, additional invoice data is entered until the match is completed. Unmatched items are transmitted to the company for clarification. Comprehensive receivables results in fewer keying errors, provides speedier updating of collections (and a shorter credit and collection process overall), and establishes a wholly automated accounts receivable system within the outsource vendor or bank.

In a recent comprehensive receivables application, revenues of a diversified manufacturing company were directed to numerous locations where office and lockbox collections were received, entered into the receivables system, and deposited. It was determined that outsourcing would develop annual savings of some $250,000.

Comprehensive Payables

Outsourcing also has been applied to disbursements through a product known as comprehensive payables. The service is initiated once a company determines that payments are owed and due, and then its bank is sent a file containing disbursement instructions. The disbursements are diaryed until the release dates specified in the file are issued in any of several mechanisms, and are funded by any money transfer arrangement chosen by the company.

As the checks are laser printed on blank safety-paper stock, the expense and risk of theft in purchasing and storing preprinted check stock is eliminated. Remittance data to show the purpose of the payment are included in the file in a specified format, printed by the bank, and attached to the check. Signatures, company logos, and other information can be printed on the check and remittance advice. Clearing payments are reconciled, and the company is provided with appropriate management information.

A public utility implemented a comprehensive payables application, developing savings of about 70 cents per transaction on an annual 250,000 transactions, worth $175,000 a year. In addition, investments in new technology were avoided, and personnel could be reassigned to other tasks.

Benefits of Payments Outsourcing

Advantages of the comprehensive receivables and payables products include the following:

- *Postage.* The U.S. Postal Service allows a "presort" discount for mail in bulk, as much as 4.5 cents less than regular first-class postage (in late 2001). Companies often are unable to access this lower postage rate due to the requirement for a high volume of mail to each receiving zip code.
- *Check signing.* The computer system of the bank maintains digitized authorized signatures. This technology eliminates

the physical signing of checks by hand or by signature plates as used on mechanical check-signing machines.

- *Company announcements.* Disbursements can include customized messages, such as "duplicate check" or "ask us about e-commerce." These announcements can be altered as payments are issued, to promote the current interests of the company.
- *Access to electronic protocols.* Electronic payments include value added networks (VANs), encryption and authentication, and complex data transmission standards. These requirements discourage many companies. Banks offer turnkey access through receivables and disbursement outsourcing, and the only prerequisite is an entry in a specific field in the file indicating the payment method.
- *Security.* Responsibility for the integrity of the payment is with the bank, so long as certain control routines are followed during the transmission of the file. The issuer need not worry about theft of live checks or checkstock, the cashing of counterfeit checks, or other security lapses.
- *Cost.* Paper processing costs about $1 to $3 per item depending on such factors as volumes, labor costs, and the extent of automation. Banks typically charge about 50 cents per item for comprehensive payables and receivables. (These cost assumptions do not include postage or other out-of-pocket expenses.) A company receiving and/or issuing 5,000 payments a month can save tens of thousands of dollars a year, while eliminating some equipment and personnel.

Outsourcing Problems

Our observation of financial outsourcing has not disclosed any significant problems with regard to the functioning of the vendor. However, there will inevitably be lapses in service quality due to changes in personnel, installation of new technology, and other factors. The most significant issue continues to be tension between the company and the outsourcer, both as an "institutional" problem and from internal resistance to change.

Confrontation Problem. Vendors are too often considered opponents rather than members in a strategic alliance. A vendor should be in a partnership relationship with the outsourcing company, which requires open communications regarding all elements of the contracted service.

Internal-Resistance-to-Change Problem. Companies have inherent internal resistance to nearly any situation involving an alteration of the organizational status quo: reorganizations; downsizing; new products, technology, or management; or even adjustments to existing business processes. Outsourcing is a special case, potentially involving all of these factors, and requiring sensitivity, a thoughtful transition, the establishment of priorities and timetables, and experienced company and outsourcer liaison.

Failures in financial outsourcing usually are traced to institutional or individual opposition rather than to the technical functioning of the product. This resistance is an important consideration in considering outsourcing, because it is one concern that is not adequately considered in the decision to proceed.

REQUEST FOR PROPOSAL

A formal request-for-proposal (RFP) process often is used to develop structured responses when considering outsourcing financial services. The typical RFP solicits answers to specific questions regarding such factors as vendor qualifications, capabilities, current clients and experience in the company's industry, disaster recovery plans, customer service procedures, and pricing. Various organizations have developed standard RFPs that may be customized to a company's specific requirements.[5]

General Information

The RFP should describe the company, including structure, lines of business, geographic locations, and the service being considered for outsourcing. Financial statements should be included as well as transaction volumes, the required timing of critical events, and the reasons for consideration of outsourcing. The outsourcer also should be informed of contracting requirements, including purchase or legal department review.

Process Description

A work flow description includes the movement of document and files through processing, the equipment and systems currently used, the process for resolving errors, and any deficiencies that outsourcing is intended to correct. The company should indicate if it wishes to be informed whenever the preformatted template or instructions for handling each activity cannot deal with a specific exception. For example, a customer may deduct a disputed amount from an invoice and remit the payment to a lockbox. How should the lockbox handle the remittance?

It is essential to indicate capabilities to send and receive information, usually through data transmission over modems or dedicated lines. Requirements for computer systems, telecommunications protocols, authentication and encryption, and the programming language should be indicated.

Pricing

A pro forma invoice often is requested to show the company the format of a typical monthly statement. This permits an advance view of the pricing structure, including all "run-rate" charges. Pricing information should include the period of the price guaranteed by the vendor, any implementation charges, and whether there are penalties for high exception or error rates or for insufficient volume.

DEVELOPMENTS IN OUTSOURCING

Additional financial outsourcing opportunities will likely include events further removed from the center of the cash flow time line; recall Exhibit 3.2. The following financial outsourcing is in development or may be offered in the future:

- Credit approvals of prospective customers based on requests from sales personnel or field offices, and slow or no payer credit and collection activities managed from data on funds received and applied to open receivables. Credit reporting agencies such as Dun & Bradstreet and Trans Union would be logical outsourcers for these services.
- Preparation of customer invoices based on files reflecting shipped orders. Several outsourcers offer invoicing services, including EDS and ADP.
- Receivables financing based on customer orders received and approved, and the collection and transfer of funds to lenders as invoices are paid. Various factors can offer this service, including GE Capital Services.
- Purchasing and accounts payable decisions based on established requirements and agreed vendor payment arrangements. National Processing Corporation (NPC) and Mellon Bank are offering this service on a limited basis.

Application Service Providers

Application service providers (ASPs) rent or lease access to, and the management of, Web-based software through central servers. These vendors offer financial applications that handle routine processing such as payroll, certain accounting functions, and ERP applications, usually based on a rental fee that can be as little as $50 or as much as $1,000 monthly. Revenues for ASPs are expected to be in the billions of dollars by the middle of the first decade of the 21st century.

The particular attraction to the ASP is the quick access to high-technology programs, with implementation often within one or two months of the "go" decision. The fee structure avoids any significant upfront charge for implementation or software licenses, and transmission security is assured by the use of the most current antivirus protections, firewalls, and other safeguards.

CONCLUSIONS

Financial outsourcers generally offer quality customer service in support of their large investments in technology and personnel. Occasionally companies are unhappy with this or that bank or vendor, but opinion is mostly favorable as to both service quality and cost. As companies search for opportunities to improve their expense management while implementing the latest technology, the outsourcing of financial functions will become an increasingly viable option.

NOTES

1. *Cashflow Reengineering* (New York: AMACOM Books, 1997), chapter 3.
2. James Sagner, "Outsourcing Disbursements," *TMA Journal* (now *AFP Exchange*) (September/October 1997), pp. 52–57.
3. Two suggested ABC references are James A. Brimson, *Activity Accounting: An Activity-Based Costing Approach* (New York: John Wiley & Sons, 1991); and Gary Cokins, *Activity-Based Cost Management* (New York: McGraw-Hill, 1996).
4. For a review of recent insourcing experiences, see Jeffrey Marshall, "Shared Services, Shared Opportunities," *Financial Executive* (July/August 2001), pp. 50–52.
5. The Association of Financial Professionals of Bethesda, MD (*www.afponline.org*) has published a three-volume set of RFPs for financial managers, *Standardized RFPs*. Services represented include controlled disbursement, depository services, retail and wholesale lockbox, wire transfer, automated clearing house (ACH), electronic data interchange (EDI), information reporting, comprehensive payables, treasury workstations, purchasing cards, merchant card, and custody.

PART 2

Financing the Corporation

Willy was a salesman . . . He's a man way out there in the blue, riding on a smile and a shoeshine. And when they start not smiling back—that's an earthquake. . . A salesman is got to dream, boy. It comes with the territory.

Arthur Miller
Death of a Salesman, "Requiem"

Access to Credit

What they taught in your MBA finance program:

Capital markets allocate funds to creditworthy businesses at reasonable cost for purposes of funding operating activities and strategic investments.

What they should have taught:

Developments in the financial markets are causing significant alterations in the traditional roles of financial institutions and their corporate clients. These changes include the rising cost of funds, the business and legal impacts of financial deregulation, and the decline in the credibility of strategic planning. As the result, traditional assumptions regarding access to funds may no longer be true.

WHAT IS CREDIT?

Lending services are provided to businesses by a variety of financial institutions, including commercial banks, securities firms, and commercial finance companies. Such credit activities may be in the form of short- or long-term loans; leases; letters of credit; the issuance of commercial paper, notes, or bonds; and various other arrangements. Credit is extended to finance both operational and investment requirements. We discussed operational activities in our review of working capital in lesson 2. This lesson focuses on longer-term uses of credit, in the financing of investment transactions.

The building block of business investment decision making traditionally has been the time value of money (TVM), which means that a dollar earned or spent today is worth more than one earned or spent in the future. The TVM is applied to capital decisions in such techniques as net present value (NPV) and internal rate of return (IRR), which use a company's cost of capital (CoC) to compare cash inflows and outflows. Projects with returns exceeding their costs, whether measured as an absolute dollar amount (as with NPV) or as an interest rate (as with IRR), are considered as appropriate for investment.

A project with an IRR of 11 percent is just acceptable when your CoC is 10 percent but should obviously be avoided if your capital costs rise to 12 percent. The CoC is the weighted cost of debt and equity used to support a company's capital structure. Here's an illustration. The balance sheet of a manufacturing company is funded one-third by debt, costing an average 9 percent, and two-thirds by equity, costing an average 14 percent. (The cost of equity capital is comprised of the expected annual growth rate of the company's stock or earnings plus the dividend yield.) The resulting weighted average 12 percent CoC is calculated in Exhibit 5.1

The low cost of capital experienced until the 1970s (about 6 percent) has vanished. We can use 1965 as the approximate border between low and escalating interest rates, driven largely by the decision of the Johnson Administration to fund its spend-

EXHIBIT 5.1   Calculation of Average Cost of Capital

	Portion of Balance Sheet (%)	Pretax Costs	After-Tax Costs	Component Costs[a]
Debt	33 1/3	.09	.06[b]	.02
Equity	66 2/3	.15[c]	.15	.10
Total	100			.12

[a]"Portion of Balance Sheet" times "After-Tax Costs."
[b]Assumes 34 percent corporate tax rate.
[c]Assumes 12.5 percent growth + 2.5 percent dividend.

ing on the Vietnam War by deficit spending rather than tax increases. From 1955 to 1964, midyear short-term interest rates (as measured by federal funds) averaged 2.5 percent, but then began an escalation that drove rates to about 5.5 percent by the year 2000.

Current Costs of Capital

The forces of supply and demand set the cost of money, in the same way that the prices of commodities are set by the action of open, competitive markets. The price of any commodity, including money, is a function of the substitutability of one commodity (bonds) for another (stocks). We care about the future trend of money rates, because as capital costs rise, a business has to reevaluate capital programs to determine if target returns are being met.

Although interest rates are down from their highs (reached at the time of the oil embargo by the Organization of Petroleum Exporting Countries [OPEC] in 1973–1974), they reflect what has occurred generally in the financial markets: capital costs that are about twice that from the post–World War II era. Total equity returns (dividends and price appreciation) averaged about 20 percent over the four-year period 1996 to 1999 and exceeded 18 percent in the decade of the 1990s.[1] The soaring stock market may have enriched most of us, at least temporarily, but it has tremendously increased the cost of equity capital.

These are not trivial costs for any business, and they appear to constitute a permanent change in the cost of financing a business. Even though inflation is mild (except for episodes of oil price increases, war, or other temporary incidents), the markets now expect a significant return for "hired" capital regardless of whether it is by a loan or a share of ownership.

Temporary Debt "Fix"

The CoC is significantly lower for debt than for equity; in our earlier example, debt capital was 9 percent pretax and 6 percent after tax, while equity capital was 15 percent. This explicit lower cost of debt capital has contributed to an increasing amount of external financing (i.e., from sources other than retained earnings), from about 10 percent in 1993 to over 15 percent by 1999 (according to Federal Reserve System statistics).

Corporations borrowed $300 billion in just the first half of 2001, compared to less than $200 billion in the previous year.[2] Chief financial officers have depended on the debt "fix" to finance their businesses, relying on financial institutions to cooperate by continuing to provide access to cheap credit. The next section explains that these sources are becoming less cooperative, and access to debt may become significantly more restricted and expensive.

The optimal amount of debt and equity on the balance sheet lies within a fairly large range, and economists refer to a U- (or saucer-) shape average cost of capital curve that shows this relationship. However, just as the bottom of the saucer cannot be extended indefinitely, there is a limit to the amount of debt U.S. corporate balance sheets can absorb. Eventually, the ability of the private sector to continue to finance its expansion is affected.

Business is constrained in its ability to generate retained earnings because of accumulated interest costs from its aggregate borrowings and the ongoing costs of labor, rent, and energy. Productivity from technology and low commodities prices supported the economic expansion of the decade of the 1990s, but these costs could not be suppressed indefinitely. The result was inevitable: an extended slowdown in capital investment and business activity.

BUSINESS IMPACT OF FINANCIAL DEREGULATION

For most of the twentieth century, U.S. financial institutions were prohibited from operating outside of their established lines of business, and commercial banks were prohibited from locating facilities outside of their state of domicile. (The McFadden Act of 1927, prohibiting interstate banking, was superceded by the Interstate Banking and Efficiency Act of 1994, which phased out McFadden restrictions by mid-1997. However, various exceptions were permitted. The Glass-Steagall Act of 1933 prohibited investment banks from engaging in most commercial banking activities.) These barriers were eliminated with the Gramm-Leach-Bliley Act of 1999, which ended all restrictions on financial service activities. By the twenty-first century, banks, securities firms, insurers, and finance companies were allowed to pursue any potentially profitable financial service activity.

With the development of sophisticated costing systems in the period after about 1980, bankers became increasingly aware that lending to large corporations did not meet their target ROE, especially compared to the fat fees broker-dealers were earning on comparable corporate finance activities. However, banks were limited in their opportunity for profitable business by legislative and regulatory barriers.

Banks Measure Profitability

According to the comedian Bob Hope, a bank is a place that will lend you money if you can prove that you don't need it. Commercial banks today are in a sellers' market for the financial needs of large corporations. They have the capital to lend or invest, and CFOs must go to them, hat in hand, and beg for consideration. Some banks are turning away borrowers, while others are demanding higher prices, more revenue, and greater returns.

We'll examine the specifics using recent data in the *Gold Sheets*.[3] An "A" rated credit requests a three-year $75 million commitment, $25 million for less than one year, and $50 million for three years. The short-term credit backs the issuance of commercial paper, which is accepted practice in that market as commercial paper is an unsecured instrument.

The profitability of bank clients is calculated through RAROC, or risk-adjusted return on capital, as required by the 1993 Basel Agreement. Various RAROC models are in use, with the general objective of determining the correct pricing for a loan, the returns from portfolios of loans, and the total risk position. By targeting risk and pricing, banks are able to increase

EXHIBIT 5.2   Typical Bank Returns in Lending Agreements

	Return before Credit Underwriting Expenses (%)[a]	Return after Credit Underwriting Expenses (%)[b]	Return with Noncredit Fee Income (%)[c]
If credit is unused	6.75	3.75	13.75
If credit is used	9.00	8.20	10.80

[a]For calculation details, see Exhibit 5.3, Section A.
[b]For calculation details, see Exhibit 5.3, Section B.
[c]For calculation details, see Exhibit 5.3 Section C.

lending income, manage their risk positions, and reject business that is marginally profitable.

Rules of thumb regarding risk-adjusted capital use a 2 percent assumption for unfunded loans greater than one year and no capital allocation for unfunded loans for less than a year. For funded loans, the capital allocation is 5 percent. The returns to the bank if the credit is used or unused are shown in Exhibit 5.2; calculation details are provided in Exhibit 5.3.

These results assume the bank's costs to underwrite the credit is $30,000 and that the profit from noncredit fee income is $50,000. Simple interest returns are calculated rather than internal rate of return (IRR), discussed in lesson 7. It is obvious that returns are unattractive—and below the cost of capital—if credit is the sole piece of business awarded to the bank. The only possibility for the bank to earn its cost of capital is if the credit is not used, if the underwriting costs are carefully managed, and, most important, if there is a substantial profit opportunity from fee income.

Several factors compound the profitability problem, including reduced operating cash flow from the slowing global economy and economic reaction to the World Trade Center and Pentagon attacks. Lenders are responding to these developments by supplementing standard contracts with covenants allowing release from funding committed credit lines. Such amendments include "material adverse change" clauses permitting escape if there has

EXHIBIT 5.3 Calculation Details for Exhibit 5.2

SECTION A

	Revenue to Bank	Calculation: Fee Times	Credit Facility	Capital Allocation	Calculation: % Capital Allocation	Times $ Allocated Capital	% Return	Calculation: $ Revenue Divided by	Capital Allocation
Not Drawn									
Short-Term	$17,500	7 bp	$25MM	$0	0%	$25MM	Infinite	$17,500	0
Long-Term	$50,000	10 bp	$50MM	$1,000,000	2%	$50MM	5.0000	$50,000	$1,000,000
Total Return							6.7500	$67,500	$1,000,000
Drawn									
Short-Term	$87,500	35 bp	$25MM	$1,250,000	5%	$25MM	7.0000	$87,500	$1,250,000
Long-Term	$250,000	50 bp	$50MM	$2,500,000	5%	$50MM	10.0000	$250,000	$2,500,000
Total Return							9.0000	$337,500	$3,750,000

SECTION B

	% Return	Calculation: $ Revenue Less Credit Expense (Profit)	Divided by Capital Allocation
Not Drawn			
Short-Term	Infinite	$2,500	$ 0
Long-Term	3.5000	$35,000	$ 1,000,000
Total Return	3.7500	$37,500	$ 1,000,000
Drawn			
Short-Term	5.8000	$72,500	$ 1,250,000
Long-Term	9.4000	$235,000	$ 2,500,000
Total Return	8.2000	$307,500	$ 3,750,000

SECTION C

	% Return	Calculation: $ Credit Profit plus Profit on Fee Business	Divided by Capital Allocation
Not Drawn			
Short-Term	Infinite	$52,500	$0
Long-Term	8.5000	$85,000	$1,000,000
Total Return	13.7500	$137,500	$1,000,000
Drawn			
Short-Term	9.8000	$122,500	$1,250,000
Long-Term	11.4000	$285,000	$2,500,000
Total Return	10.8667	$407,500	$3,750,000

Notes: bp = basis points; MM = millions. Calculated amounts in text boxes. Drawn credit facilities display fee income for 3 years. Interest calculated as simple interest, without regard to the time value of money.

been a substantial injurious development in the financial position of the borrower.

"Subsidization" by Noncredit Products

Lending was "subsidized" for much of the 1980s and 1990s by large returns from other financial institution business segments, including retail banking and corporate noncredit products (see lesson 6), whose ROEs often exceeded 15 or 20 percent. However, by the late 1990s, competition and hard negotiation by corporations drove pricing down to where banks were earning only marginal returns on commercial banking, forcing them to abandon unprofitable activities. As one example, many banks have exited the retail lockbox business, and specialized vendors, such as EDS, GTE, National Processing Company, Associates Commerce Solutions, and Fiserv, have taken their position.

Retail lockbox is a collection mechanism in which mail containing payments bypasses corporate offices, going directly to a post office box maintained by the bank of deposit, thereby reducing collection float. After deposit of the check, remittance advices, photocopies of the check, and other supporting material are forwarded to the corporate credit department. Automated processing captures encoded MICR (magnetic ink character recognition) and/or OCR (optical character recognition) information on the bottom of the check and/or remittance documents and transmits it to the client in a data file.

Profitability analyses by customer, line of business, and geographic division is proprietary information. However, it is generally recognized that target returns can be met only in certain customer situations, including middle market and small corporates lending, and consumer transactions including credit card, mergers and acquisitions, and venture capital. For example, Bank One's chairman, James Dimon, is in the process of dropping corporate customers who want to borrow but do not provide sufficient fee revenues to make loans profitable,[4] and ABN-AMRO, a large Dutch multinational, has announced its intention to reduce its investment in the commercial banking business.[5]

In the scramble for profitable business, many strategic mistakes have been made, including retail banking problems (i.e., Bank One's First USA credit card business[6]), venture capital losses (i.e., at J. P. Morgan Chase[7]), small business loan problems (i.e., at First Union[8]), and financial products problems (i.e., derivatives at Bankers Trust[9]). Banks have made countless bad ("nonperforming") loans, have entered into questionable mergers, have fired tens of thousands of employees, and have introduced unpopular business practices to improve profits, such as charging for teller and ATM services.

Case of the Disappearing Credit

Chief financial officers are increasingly facing a chilly reception when they seek new sources of funding. An industry survey indicated that bank lending, recently half of all corporate borrowings, is expected to be down to about 37 percent in 2001.[10] Some banks are still working through significant losses in corporate lending.[11] And the long-time safety valve, Japanese banks, no longer provide credit facilities at nominal cost because of their own economic problems.

Syndicated lending—jumbo loans typically placed by money center banks that are resold to other financial institutions and large investors—has declined by more than 60 percent in just the past three years. Banks are tightening lending standards, are attempting to manage their troubled loan portfolios, and are using scarce lending capital to honor outstanding line-of-credit commitments. Many business loans now are written for just under one year's duration to meet international bank capital standards, and recent Federal Reserve Board statistics show that short-term loans exceed long-term loans by more than 20 times.[12]

The result is that CFOs are becoming the "Willy Lomans"[13] of the financial world, traveling with their road shows to sell their "stories" to rating agencies, lenders, investment bankers, and journalists. Because of the reluctance of banks to accept credit business, the number of potential credit contacts has had to be increased significantly, sweetened by promises to reassign noncredit business from longtime relationship banks.

In one case, a New York Stock Exchange–listed company that enjoyed a 100-year relationship with a money center bank was told that a line of credit would no longer be available, despite an investment-grade rating and a superior balance sheet. Credit lines are used both as standby sources of credit and as support for the issuance of commercial paper. In this situation, as with many Fortune 100 companies, the credit line backed commercial paper issuance, which funds the liquidity requirements of the company. Lower-tier banks in the relationship provided some relief, but the desired aggregated credit was not attained.

What Will Banks Do with Their Capital?

Bank capital will almost certainly pursue diversification opportunities, emulating the Citigroup (Citicorp/Travelers) merger (1998), which now includes such companies as Salomon Smith Barney and Associates First Capital. These deals will be relatively easy to strike among banks, diversified financial service companies, and securities firms, given the ROEs of banks (15 percent), diversified financials (18 percent), and securities firms (19 percent). They will be harder to make for insurance companies, which have an average ROE of 9 percent.[14]

The motivations for these megadeals include the elimination of costs; the enhanced opportunities for the cross-selling of products; and the opportunity to diversify portfolio risk.

The Elimination of Costs.   Increased returns are expected by scrapping such duplicate costs as systems, offices, staff, and marketing and by the control of prices charged as the industry emerges into oligopolies from its current posture of significant competition. However, businesses may be acquired in which the acquirer has no real expertise and/or where a clash of cultures may be a serious impediment. Two examples: insurers like State Farm, AIG, Met Life, and Allstate, which are moving into banking; and Prudential Insurance, which has struggled with its acquisition of Bache Securities (now Prudential Securities) in 1981.[15]

Opportunities for Cross-Selling. Complementary marketing prospects will be significant as the largest companies can offer a nearly complete array of financial services to corporate and individual customers. However, various studies have shown that the average bank customer currently buys only about two products, and some banks offer customization for their priority corporate customers, resulting in the creation of unique and costly products.[16]

Portfolio Risk Diversification. Financial institutions will be able to better diversify their asset holdings to reduce portfolio risk and more accurately predict the expected enterprise return. A large, globally diversified financial services company may be able to generate an almost risk-free return. As the result, it can fulfill its commitments to meet highly liquid claims—such as those associated with demand deposit (checking) accounts—with little price or capital risk, enhancing its attractiveness to potential investors and business partners.

LEGAL IMPACT OF FINANCIAL DEREGULATION

The legal impact of deregulation remains to be resolved in the U.S. Congress or in the courts. Will megadeals be allowed, potentially hindering competition and restricting corporate access to traditional banking services? An appropriate parallel may be the Microsoft decision by District Court Judge Thomas P. Jackson, as modified by the appeals court.[17] The central issue of the Department of Justice's case was whether competition had been hampered and innovation discouraged by the company's behavior and de facto market position. This is an important concern for the management of financial institutions, as mergers the size of Citigroup could be interpreted as hampering competition.

Issues in the Microsoft Case

A major focus of developing technology is entry to bank and vendor systems through the Internet. Ironically, a central charge in the Justice Department case is that Microsoft illegally tied its

Web browser to its Windows operating system, even though a 1998 federal appeals court ruling held that the company had the right to integrate new features into Windows if there were some consumer benefit. Thus, at the moment when the use of e-commerce connectivity would lower banking costs and extend access to multiple corporate users (i.e., the operating business users), the court contended that this is harmful behavior.

The years of litigation finally ended with a settlement in November 2001 that seems—in the opinion of many observers—to favor Microsoft. The agreement struck with the Justice Department does not affect the development or design of products or aggressive marketing strategies. Microsoft is prohibited from bullying its business rivals and partners, and some technical information must be disclosed. Perhaps most significant is the apparent reluctance of the appeals court and the government to restrict software design specifically and innovation generally.

Old Economy Antitrust

Antitrust has been national policy since the Sherman Act of 1890 and the Clayton Act of 1914, as extended and amplified by a series of laws and court decisions. The concepts of the restraint of trade and monopoly (sections 1 and 2 of the Sherman Act) have been applied generally to manufacturing companies, where economies of scale preclude easy entry to markets.

In the first important industrial case, decided in 1911, Standard Oil was convicted of driving competitors out of business and having monopolized the production and distribution of petroleum products. The U.S. government had to intervene or Standard Oil could have restrained market entry to competitors while charging customers any price it desired. The result was the dissolution of Standard Oil and the fostering of competition, which benefited everyone.[18]

The leading case involving a "nonindustrial" organization was AT&T, considered by most observers to be a telecommunications company. However, the same economies-of-scale issues occur in that industrial sector, and the company had long been a protected "natural" monopoly. AT&T was broken up into seven "Baby Bell" operating companies in 1983.[19]

New Economy Antitrust

The underlying issues in the Microsoft case are whether the company has prevented competition and innovation in the development and commercialization of computer products and whether the prices charged to customers are predatory. No quantitative evidence has been presented to show that Microsoft's dominance has adversely affected the computer industry or the consumer. For example, Netscape and Microsoft competed, improved products, distributed millions of free programs, and sustained the growth of the Internet.

What outcome would maximize economic efficiency? Will we experience productivity increases and lower prices if Microsoft had been split into multiple companies, as the courts demanded? There is clear evidence that old economy monopolists (i.e., Standard Oil) harmed customers by controlling the supply of product to keep prices high. In contrast, new economy entrepreneurs are flooding their markets with free or nominally priced products to gain market share.

The industrial monopoly of the old manufacturing economy may no longer be the relevant paradigm for the new economy based on finance and information. Such markets may be more similar to the "natural" monopolies formerly presumed to foster the optimal outcome in industries requiring huge initial capital investments. Old economy natural monopolies (e.g., electric power, water, telephone service) were closely regulated by federal or state agencies, and changes in rates and service had to be approved by those bodies.

However, the outcome was often the subsidization of one class of service by others, inefficient operations, and poor decision making. In fact, the current trend is toward deregulation, as evidenced by the elimination of airline pricing by the old

Civil Aeronautics Board, the expansion of energy utilities into distant markets, and competition in telephone service.

Does Antitrust Apply to Banking?

The tremendous economic growth of the past two decades has involved innovations in manufacturing, finance, and marketing; the introduction of new products and services; and the development of international markets. The U.S. government has fostered this expansion by supporting global industrialization, avoiding restrictive regulation and control, and allowing companies like Microsoft to standardize operating system protocols.

Congress has not passed significant antitrust legislation since the Celler-Kefauver Act of 1950 (to include asset acquisitions to augment section 7 of the 1914 Clayton Act prohibiting stock acquisitions which lessen competition). This silence has allowed policy to default to a common law, case-specific evolution of antitrust doctrine through the mechanism of the federal courts. The courts likely will be reluctant to interfere in business decisions for fear of impeding the development of product and technology. The resolution of the Microsoft case may induce future financial service merger and acquisition activity to continue the trend to consolidation as long as innovation is fostered and competitive behavior is not unduly affected.

DISAPPEARING BANKERS

The developments discussed in this lesson have dampened the enthusiasm of the capital markets in their traditional support of business investment. Lenders now have numerous attractive uses for scarce funds and are supporting activities that have fast payoffs, with accretive results often by the end of the first year. Chief financial officers had never faced a credit "drought," and in past years were wined and dined for the favor of their business. Those days are over, quite possibly forever, although few companies are prepared to face the disappearance of their bankers.

Even Fortune 1000 companies are discovering that fewer banks means a shortage of lenders, forcing a reduction in or changes to financing arrangements. This development is causing distress to the commercial paper market, which is dependent on bank credit line backing as a guarantee for its unsecured short-term borrowing. As the result, some CFOs are proactively changing their capital structures to reduce their commercial paper positions, by issuing long-term debt and other strategies.

It is unlikely that Congress or the regulators will force banks to lend to creditworthy borrowers. Assuming "benign neglect" in the credit markets, CFOs must consider and promote nontraditional alternatives to traditional loan sources. Such alternatives include:

- *Capital rationing.* As noted at the beginning of this chapter, corporate finance teaches that any project with an IRR higher than its CoC (or with a positive net present value) should be funded. However, in an atmosphere of strict capital rationing, an acceptable level of total investment is determined and projects then are funded based on returns, criticality to the mission of the company, and any other extenuating circumstances (e.g., regulatory or safety requirements or the impending obsolescence of an existing asset).
- *Strategic alliances.* Partnering with competitors or companies in allied industries is becoming an accepted approach to developing a new product, conducting research, entering a new market, or pursuing any activity involving a capital investment. Various factors support strategic alliances, including globalization, the shedding of noncore competencies, the need for rapid response to e-commerce opportunities,[20] and a generally accommodative antitrust policy. As the result, alliances and partnerships are becoming viable alternatives to acquiring or building.
- *Commercial finance lending.* Commercial finance has evolved into a $1 trillion industry, with business loans

primarily based on equipment, receivables, or other collateral. Such loans traditionally have been to subpar borrowers at higher-than-bank rates, including venture finance loans to early-stage high-technology and other subpar companies at interest rates of up to 20 percent. However, given the tightening bank credit market, some borrowers may be forced to accept loans and the higher rates offered by commercial finance companies.

- *Innovative financing.* Companies must work with banks to redesign traditional lending products. Leveraged buyouts (LBOs), the commercial paper dealer and direct issuance, derivatives, and other financial products were developed in the last three decades in response to market demand. Similarly, CFO demand for credit will force lenders to offer adequate lending facilities to enable business to continue to operate, while generating adequate profits for all parties.

CONCLUSIONS

The old assumptions about creditworthy businesses having ready access to capital at reasonable cost is changing to one of the CFO as a supplicant, pleading for a loan. Banks perceive that they make more money on other products than commercial lending, and may restrict access to scarce funds accordingly. The successful financial manager must arrange for funding from various sources and pursue other "nonfinance" strategies.

NOTES

1. For large company stocks, the 1980s average was 17.5 percent. See *Stocks, Bonds, Bills and Inflation, 2000 Yearbook* (Chicago, IL: Ibbotson Associates, 2000), Table 1-1, p. 19.
2. "Corporate America's Big Debt to the Fed," *BusinessWeek,* May 28, 2001, pp. 88–89, at 88.

3. Data are from late August 2001. The *Gold Sheets,* a publication of Loan Pricing Corp./ Reuters (*www.loanpricing.com*), provide analyses of market trends in the global syndicated loan and high-yield bond markets, including coverage of pricing, structure, tenor, and industry segments.

4. See "Can Jamie Dimon Win at Cards?" *BusinessWeek,* April 23, 2001, pp. 94–95.

5. See Alan Cowell, "ABN Amro Shifts Focus Back to Traditional Banking," *New York Times,* August 17, 2001, p. W1.

6. See "A Panic over Plastic," *BusinessWeek,* September 6, 1999, pp. 32–33, updated in "Bank One: Out of Excuses?" *BusinessWeek,* January 24, 2000, pp. 52–54.

7. See "A Rough Patch for Chase's VC [venture capital] Unit Rocks the Parent's Earnings," *BusinessWeek,* November 6, 2000, p. 194.

8. See "How the Money Store Became a Money Pit," *BusinessWeek,* July 10, 2000, p. 62.

9. See "The Bankers Trust Tapes," *BusinessWeek,* October 16, 1995, pp. 106–111.

10. "AFP Survey Shows Shift in Credit Resources," *AFP Pulse,* February 2000, pp. 1, 7.

11. See "Is Wachovia's Plight a Warning?" *BusinessWeek,* July 3, 2000, p. 40.

12. $87.5 billion versus $4.2 billion, reported in "Terms of Lending at Commercial Banks," *Federal Reserve Bulletin,* August 2001, Table 4.23.A.

13. Willy Loman is the protagonist of Arthur Miller's classic play, *Death of a Salesman* (1949).

14. The weighted average ROE for the insurance companies reported in Fortune categories 31 and 33, including life and health mutual and stock companies, and property and casualty mutual and stock companies. ROEs reported directly include: banks, industry no. 9; diversified financials, no. 14; and securities firms, no. 51. "Fortune 500 Issue," *Fortune Magazine,* April 16, 2001, pp. F-45–F-68.

15. Two articles that discussed the cultural problems in this merger were: "Not So Prudent," *The Economist,* August 31, 1991, pp. 59–60; and Terence P. Pare, "Scandal Isn't All That Ails the Pru," *Fortune Magazine,* March 21, 1994, pp. 52–56.

16. From studies by Booz, Allen & Hamilton and First Union; cited in "Empty Aisles at the Financial Supermarket," *BusinessWeek,* November 8, 1999, p. 40.

17. See "Conclusions of Law", in *U.S. v. Microsoft* 97 F. Supp. 2d 59, 63 (2000), and reported in "Company Found to Have Abused Monopoly

Power," *New York Times,* April 4, 2000, pp. C14–C15. The district court found that Microsoft monopolized the market for operating systems by mounting "a deliberate assault upon entrepreneurial efforts that . . . could well have enabled the introduction of competition" (at Section I.A. III. C., p. C15).

18. *Standard Oil of NJ v. U.S.,* 221 U.S.1 (1911).

19. *U.S. v. Western Electric Co.,* 569 F. Supp. 1057 (1983); Aff'd *sub. nom., California v. U.S.,* 464 U.S. 1013 (1983).

20. See James Sagner, *Financial and Process Metrics for the New Economy* (New York: AMACOM Books, 2001), chapters 2 and 3.

Noncredit Banking Services

What they taught in your MBA finance program:

Banks offer a range of noncredit services to corporate borrowers at reasonable prices to complement their lending activities.

What they should have taught:

Just as banks are deemphasizing corporate lending (see lesson 5), noncredit service offerings are being fully priced or will no longer be offered.

WHAT ARE NONCREDIT SERVICES?

"Noncredit services" include a wide variety of functions performed for businesses other than lending. The list of services, performed primarily by commercial banks, includes domestic and international cash management, foreign exchange, securities custody, trust services, and trade finance. These and other activities essentially support the transactional requirements of business, allowing the efficient movement of goods, funds, and information between buyers and sellers.

When we talk about commercial banking at the start of the twenty-first century, we are really addressing the 8,500 or so places where deposits are accepted and loans are made. Only a small portion of those institutions is active to any significant extent in noncredit corporate services. The rest of the banks deal primarily with the needs of local retail consumers and small to medium-size businesses. Our U.S. banking structure included some 15,000 commercial banks as recently as the mid-1980s, primarily because of federal restrictions on interstate banking and restrictions in some states on branch banking (e.g., Illinois). With the ending of these barriers, the commercial bank population has declined by about 43 percent.[1]

In cash management, a recent survey notes that the consolidation in banking has nearly doubled in five years, with the largest banks controlling 47 percent of cash management revenue compared to 27 percent in 1994.[2] This group of five banks will average $800 million in domestic activity this year, with the next group of five banks having revenues of $300 million and banks 11 to 15 having revenue of $200 million. The banking industry is clearly moving toward an oligopolistic structure from one of substantial competition in noncredit services.

What does this mean for CFOs who must continuously monitor their banking fees and activities? Does oligopoly mean lower or higher prices? Faster or slower technological innovation? In other words, what does the future hold?

PRICING OF BANK NONCREDIT SERVICES

Emerging oligopolies occur in industries that have been deregulated, such as the airlines and the securities industry, and in maturing industries where economies of scale drive efficiencies, such as the automobile industry in the 1930s. Prices in emerging oligopolies typically increase slightly faster than general inflation (as measured by the Producer Price Index, or PPI), as the transition from more intense competition allows greater control over prices charged and profits earned. If customers refuse to support such a pricing policy, products that cannot achieve a target return may be abandoned. Thus, airlines raise prices, eliminate routes and hubs, and reduce such services as meals.

Pricing data from the Phoenix-Hecht website shows Blue Book price performance over the most recent four-year period. The average price increase was 2.6 percent, with more manual products experiencing increases of about 5.5 percent.[3] This increase exceeds the recent performance of business inflation as measured by the PPI/finished goods index, which was 1.5 percent in mid-2001.[4]

In fact, the price increases experienced would be considerably greater if the world's economy were not facing the very real prospect of recession, limiting any price increases banks could impose. For example, industrial production in the European Union (EU) countries fell an annualized 2.7 percent through late 2001, with the U.S. down 5.9 percent and Japan down 13.1 percent.[5]

As we noted in lesson 5, banks today have to assign scarce dollars among several alternative choices, including merger and acquisition (M&A) activity; post-M&A worker separation and site closure/integration costs; and investments in technology, employee compensation, and product and quality initiatives. Corporate customers are finding that their banks' profits are being used more for M&A and less for other activities, with technological development clearly not as important as in the early part of this decade.

Management of Banking Costs

Because it will take decades for these economic structure issues to be resolved, the CFO must be vigilant in managing bank costs. The following three steps seem prudent:

1. Review all bank services to be certain that the corporation is using and needs the services being purchased. For example, a financial services company encouraged the development of separate organizations by each of its business units, without the benefit of input from and expertise of the other businesses. Decisions on most purchases and investments were made by each business with little input from the relevant staff unit. One business decided to have its disbursement bank do special processing on its 150,000 monthly cleared checks, including sorts to

lines of business. The bank agreed, but charged as much for the special processing as for basic controlled disbursement! Reengineering this process saved in excess of $70,000 annually.

2. Continually monitor prices charged, comparing account analyses costs to prices offered by various providers. (An "account analysis" is a commercial bank's invoice for services provided to corporate customers.) For example, a consumer products company used the same banks for cash management services for many years, depending on the banks to deal fairly on pricing. On close examination, it was determined that charges were an average of 20 percent too high. Changes eventually resulted in the company, saving annually in excess of $50,000.

3. Consider banking relationships as a bundled combination of credit and noncredit activities of mutual benefit to both the company and the bank(s). In one case, a commercial bank provided credit to a large corporation but received no other business from it. After several years of trying to sell noncredit fee services, the bank finally pulled its credit line. To make the banker-corporation relationship mutually beneficial, banks must derive adequate credit *and* noncredit revenues.

BANK TECHNOLOGY

Many CFOs are worried that innovation in financial technology will be stifled by a developing oligopolistic structure. Industries with a limited number of sellers may support investments in technology if a competitive advantage is likely to result *or* in response to a competitor's action, but they also abandon rather quickly products that cannot attain a "fair" return. Only a handful of banks still offer such services as foreign exchange, derivatives, and other products.

For illustrative purposes, bank technology development is discussed using electronic data interchange (EDI) and its emerging companion e-commerce (electronic commerce). EDI began in the United States with the organization of the X-12 committee by the American National Standards Institute (ANSI) in 1978, allowing companies to communicate electronically to place orders, invoice, and authorize payments.[6] E-commerce extends the technology interface to include the Internet, to permit access to electronics without the cost, rigidity, or expertise required of EDI.

EDI/E-Commerce "Product"

The banks that jumped into EDI by the mid-1980s—including First National Bank of Chicago/NBD (now Bank One), Mellon, Citibank, Chase Manhattan (now J. P. Morgan Chase), Bank of America, and Northern Trust—built a commanding position. They became value-added banks (VABs), providing numerous bells and whistles beyond the basic service, and are now in "partner" relationships with their Fortune 1000 clients.

Such services include separating and reassociating payment and remittance information, with the remittance sent to the trading partner's bank either electronically or by paper and the payment sent through the ACH. Following reassociation, the payment and remittance are transmitted to the company. In addition, VABs can merge and transmit all types of payments, including EDI/e-commerce, checks, ACHs, wires, and credit/debit card payments through an EDI/e-commerce or proprietary format. Typical EDI/e-commerce services provided by VABs are shown in Exhibit 6.1.

In contrast, basic-service banks provide a "plain-vanilla" EDI/e-commerce product: for example, receiving and sending payment and payment-related EDI/e-commerce information either directly or through a value-added network. Several regional banks can be considered as basic service: National City, Key Bank, Allfirst Bank, and PNC. According to a recent survey, middle-market companies—those typically serviced by such banks—are unlikely to currently have EDI/e-commerce. However, they are beginning to face the same counterparty requests and demands for EDI/e-commerce as larger organizations and

EXHIBIT 6.1   Typical VAB EDI/E-Commerce Services

*Electronic messages and confirmations.

are beginning to consider the outsourcing of EDI/e-commerce related activities, such as disbursements and electronic bill presentment and payment (EBPP).[7]

Implementation Processes

Basic-service banks may not have a standard set of protocols in establishing an EDI/e-commerce client. Often procedures do not exist to guide the sale, implementation, or operational efforts necessary to enable a satisfactory EDI/e-commerce relationship. The absence of such procedures can lead to delays and cost overruns with clients.

VABs typically use a very structured approach to implementation, including GANTT charts and milestone deadlines. Typical steps include:

- Assignment of dedicated implementation team
- Review of internal client systems
- Determination of existing EDI/e-commerce and transmission capabilities
- Analysis of security requirements
- Mapping of data from client proprietary files to bank formats

- Development of implementation guide
- Review of technical issues
  —File formats
  —Platform compatibilities
  —Communications profiles
  —Acknowledge protocols
- Management of administrative issues
  —Legal contracts
  —Funding procedures
  —The handling of returned items
  —Operating procedures
  —Training of client personnel
  —Service agreements

Other Differences

Regular channels of communications may be missing between customers and the various organizational elements within basic-service banks. Customer demands, "emergencies," and sensitivities may drive activities regardless of profitability or bank priorities. VABs use a structured approach to ensure communication between all affected parties and manage pressure points by reference to their standard implementation and customer service procedures.

Basic-service banks generally do not use sophisticated technology in product delivery. For example, the operating system used for some electronic transactions may be on a DOS platform, technology made obsolete more than a decade ago by the Windows operating system. In comparison, EDI/e-commerce VAB banks operate Windows-based EDI/e-commerce systems, and some are transitioning from mainframe systems to servers and networks.

The development of advanced technology for cash management services will be limited to those VABs that can afford the investment and foresee profit potential in new delivery mechanisms. Basic-service banks will offer plain-vanilla products to less demanding companies, largely the middle market.

The result: The emerging oligopoly in cash management banking will reduce the number of providers of advanced technological services.

VENDOR TECHNOLOGY

Nonbank vendors have entered nearly every area of service as banks reduce their cash management offerings. Some 225 exhibitors operate booths at the annual conference of the Association of Financial Professionals, with elaborate displays offering everything from automobiles to computers for "lucky" lottery winners.

There are now about 175 nonbank vendors, and the percentage of bank exhibitors has dropped from 30 percent in 1993 to 20 percent in 2001. Vendors offer all types of treasury services, from "we do everything" to various niche providers. In trying to understand the evolving role of nonbank vendors, we will focus on one bank/vendor product used by many companies, the treasury information system (TIS).

Evolution of Treasury Information Systems

Data on daily bank activity was first electronically transmitted on "dumb terminals." The treasury analyst placed the phone in a cradle in the computer terminal, dialed up, and received a download of debits, credits, and one-day and two-day availability. Little customization was required for clients to receive this transmission, and the banks could provide a useful product, recover their costs, and capture their customers in a semipermanent relationship.

Once a demand for online treasury reporting had been confirmed by customer acceptance, newer versions of the product were developed. Banks identified a market need, created a prototype, worked with beta (test) sites, developed a production version, and provided limited customization. The information products of banks during the 1990s were largely continuations of 1980s' concepts with significant technological innovations. Various product features were added, such as Windows for older DOS systems, processing for more sophisticated instruments such as derivatives, and encryption and authentication for security.[8]

Trouble started when financial managers began to demand more sophisticated products. The idea of a stand-alone treasury workstation—as this product came to be called—seemed inadequate. Deficiencies included the requirement for repetitive keying to other systems, the need to create company-specific spreadsheets, and the lack of analytical tools. A monster had been created, and banks had to respond before their competitors would seize the initiative (and their customers).

Treasury Information System Interfaces with Other Systems

The result was ill-advised investments in treasury management products with various modules and interfaces. Consider a few of the functions that these systems attempted to provide in addition to plain-vanilla bank transaction reporting and money movement:

- Links to various internal/external systems including accounts receivable and accounts payable
- Mapping of repetitive transactions to automate journal entries
- Cash forecasting
- Risk management
- Money market sales/investments
- Rate feeds from data services (e.g., Bloomberg, Reuters) to mark derivatives to market to calculate value-at-risk
- Global transactions including foreign exchange
- Roll-up of positions from regional treasury centers
- In-house bank for multinationals including netting

Exhibit 6.2 shows the schematic of an integrated treasury management system.

The central cash management system is supported by live data from sales (for receivables) and purchases (for payables), with feeds to accounting for recurring cash-related transactions

EXHIBIT 6.2   Integrated Treasury Management System Schematic

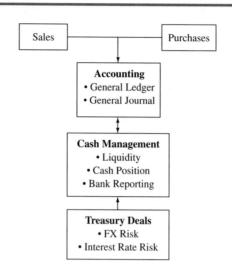

whenever and wherever they occur and for occasional treasury "deals." The interactions and operations are of staggering complexity, considering that a change to any one factor would potentially ripple through to all other system components. (Scientists have studied these phenomena in the context of chaos theory.)

These products were supposed to do everything, be user friendly and be easy to install, but not cost a lot more than the early versions of the product, because, after all, banks don't charge much for noncredit services. The problem was that these enhancements required enormous development and implementation costs, along with systems professionals to maintain the product.

Treasury Information System Vendors Seize the Market

As noted earlier, economic theory would suggest that the emergence of an oligopolistic cash management banking structure would lead to the abandonment of products that disappoint customers and lose money. And that's exactly what has happened. A recent review of the treasury system product cited only two bank providers, J. P. Morgan Chase and Bank of America.[9] Other banks sell more basic cash management systems or simply decline to talk about their products.

The nonbank vendors have jumped into this market with sophisticated, multifunctional products. And, as economic theory would predict, the traditional pricing of these products has changed totally. Companies such as SAP, PeopleSoft, and SunGard are charging well into six figures, an unheard of amount back in the days of $10,000 to $15,000 pricing.

These vendors are providing consulting services to assist in the analysis of requirements, integration with legacy systems, general ledger interface, implementation, and training. In other words, they are offering complete packages of services that banks simply cannot supply. Of course, if a company cannot afford this level of investment, basic-service offerings from banks are priced closer to traditional levels.

IMPACT ON BANK NONCREDIT SERVICES

In responding to this changing environment, banks are pursuing several actions to rationalize the marketing of noncredit services.

Market Definition

As bankers develop sophisticated profitability models, they will be able to determine contributions by customer, industry, product, and geographic segment. These data then can be used to define appropriate target markets with input from lending groups, capital markets groups, and other banking areas. This is a critical business strategy, because a banking institution cannot sell to every possible prospect. Instead, the focus will be on profitable opportunities with reasonable growth potential.

One approach is to develop a rating system or decision tree to qualify corporate prospects during precalling and calling. Bankers must be selective in determining viable calling opportunities. While the process of scoring or rating prospects is specific to each bank, often the following variables are considered:

- The CFO's general satisfaction with his or her current banks and their calling officers, including credit and noncredit products
- Current banks' capabilities in quality assurance, customer service, disaster recovery, pricing, technology, and other general factors
- The efficiency of the prospect in managing its financial activities
- Loyalty of the prospect to existing banks, based on the length of the relationship, any senior management or board of directors relationships, geographic allegiance, or other factors
- Potential business activity, based on current transaction volumes

Chief Financial Officer's Priorities

Bankers are becoming more focused on the needs of and the incentives driving the CFO. While CFO has been the final authority for the purchase of banking services through most of the past decade, often he or she has been willing to defer the selection to the treasurer or assistant treasurer. With the downsizing of financial staff and the emphasis on the capital structure of the business, the CFO is seizing the buying decision while continuing to focus on those issues that matter to him or her: corporate finance and capital markets.

Simply put, the CFO does not much care about, and is not paid to think about, noncredit services. If a CFO of a $100 million company can reduce annual funding costs by 25 basis points, the annual savings are $250,000. It is hard to conceive of noncredit service efficiencies that can possibly have such an impact. Furthermore, bank noncredit service salespeople cannot talk about credit or capital market issues, and so will not be of much help to the company in providing advice on economic trends or financing alternatives.

Educating Calling Officers

Banks are educating their calling officers (or relationship managers) to recognize and promote selling opportunities for their complex sets of products. Until about the mid-1980s, all credit, capital markets, and noncredit service products were presented to the corporate customer by a single individual, the calling officer. Many money center and regional banks then realized that noncredit services required a separate sales force to receive appropriate attention and promotion. As a result, the dual selling by banks created different calling levels: the CFO (and treasurer) for credit and capital markets and the assistant treasurer and other staff for noncredit products.

This was an effective strategy so long as noncredit management products were relatively simple, independent, and inexpensive to use. However, the increasing use of technology and the integration of bank and company systems has caused the development of more sophisticated products, requiring greater financial analysis, technological skills for implementation and operation, an understanding of corporate issues that extend beyond finance, and a sensitivity for corporate political and personnel issues.

Examples of this development are comprehensive receivables and payables, described in lesson 4. These products have ramifications for various functional areas in a company, including finance, purchasing, accounts payable, audit, and information systems. Because of the products' broad sweep, a sale requires the involvement of a senior manager—the CFO—and normally that person is not called on by the bank noncredit salesperson.

Deemphasis of Noncredit Selling

Banks are deemphasizing the role of the noncredit sales force. Existing noncredit salespeople market standard sets of mature, stand-alone products, with little hope of extending these products into additional marketing opportunities. The trend in banking and in the corporation-banker relationship is for the consolidation to a few, very important relationships. This consolidation cannot be accomplished unless the calling officer is highly consultative, able to reach senior financial managers, and capable of offering a full range of banking services.

Many noncredit salespeople are focused entirely on the sale of product and frequently do not exhibit advisory skills, do not understand credit issues, and usually do not deal with senior corporate managers. The era of selling cash management, custody, and other noncredit services as separate products is clearly ending. Banks are beginning to prepare for this development by selectively deemphasizing noncredit sales and reassigning these responsibilities.

CONCLUSIONS

Banks no longer consider noncredit services as an obligatory complement to lending, as profit pressures are forcing price increases or the abandonment of markets previously served. CFOs are being forced to partner with their banks to enable them to make reasonable returns. In addition, vendor products will have to be considered for selected noncredit services.

NOTES

1. As of the end of 1999, 8,620 banks were in operation; reported in "Profits and Balance Sheet Developments in U.S. Commercial Banks in 1999," *Federal Reserve Bulletin,* June 2000, pp. 367–395, at 368.
2. Reported as "1998 Ernest & Young Cash Management Survey," *TMA Journal* (now *AFP Exchange*), September/October 1998, pp. 40–46.
3. Phoenix-Hecht (*www.phoenixhecht.com*) is an independent cash management advisory firm that specializes in mail time surveys, lockbox collection, and clearing float analysis computer models. The data are from the 2000–2001 "Blue Book of Bank Prices" survey.
4. Reported at the website of the U.S. Department of Labor, Bureau of Labor Statistics, *stats.bls.gov,* for the year ending July 2001.

5. Reported in *The Economist*, "Economic and Financial Indicators," January 5, 2002, p. 84.

6. See the Data Interchange Standards Association website, *www.disa.org*. An important published reference on electronic data interchange is Thomas P. Colberg, ed., *The Price Waterhouse EDI Handbook* (New York: John Wiley & Sons, 1995).

7. "Incentives and Barriers to Electronic Payments," *TMA Journal* (now *AFP Exchange*), July/August 1998, pp. 34–41.

8. See Nicholas Mitsos, "Vertical Integration in Global Treasury Management," *TMA Journal* (now *AFP Exchange*), November/December 1998, pp. 78–81.

9. Richard Gamble, "The Big Buzz in Treasury Workstations," *Business Finance*, November 1998, pp. 44–51.

Strategic Planning and Capital Budgeting

What they taught in your MBA finance program:

Capital budgeting procedures support strategic planning.

What they should have taught:

Strategic planning and capital budgeting are dependent on flawed long-term assumptions about costs, future cash inflows, costs of capital, and event probabilities. The techniques in general use are mathematically correct but misleading in their appearance of precision and logic.

WHAT IS STRATEGIC PLANNING?

The essence of strategic planning is the integration of decisions regarding a company's future business operations, including operational activities and capital investments. Operations include decisions on products, channels of distribution, pricing, and the deployment of employees. For this lesson we are more interested in investment activities, including buying or building plant, equipment, technology, or other capital assets.

Access to the financial markets supports business operational and investment activities. Operational requirements are analyzed by perusing budgets, financial statements, ratios, and other working capital drivers (see lesson 2). Investment requirements are more tenuous and depend on forecasts of such factors as customer demand, actions of competitors, the cost and revenues of the project over a future time horizon, and the company's cost of capital (CoC).

The synthesis of the elements of an investment has been the responsibility of strategic planning, whether conducted as a stand-alone business function, as part of the office of the chief executive officer, or by consultants. Regardless, finance and the CFO play critical roles in strategic planning, in determining the CoC to evaluate investment proposals, in developing sources of capital, and in deciding whether the whole process is so conjectural as to be nonsense. Unfortunately, however, many companies allow their organization's planning function to make critical (and often flawed) financial assumptions when capital investments are budgeted.

Early Trends in Strategic Planning

There have been various fads in strategic planning, many of which began with a focus on vision. The concept is that for a company to survive and prosper, it must continually redefine its products, markets, and potential customers. A vision may include reassembling the basic foundation of the organization to meet newly prescribed business conditions. This is not a new idea; an early comment on the subject of defining a market was by Theodore Levitt.[1] His focus was on the needs of the customer versus the sale of product.

The decades of the 1960s and 1970s saw a significant rise in the popularity of strategic planning. Companies looking past the post–World War II boom used formalized planning to prevent business from merely attempting to continue its past successes, to take advantage of new technologies and global markets, and to bring a decorum and quasi-professionalism to what had generally been an informal process.

The leading gurus included Boston Consulting Group, Booz Allen and Hamilton, and other strategic consulting firms. One popular message was that all business sectors could be classified as stars, cows, dogs, and question marks (or a similar nomenclature). The meaning of these terms was fairly obvious: fund the stars (or potential stars), milk the cash cows but provide only the essential additional investment, eliminate the dogs, and investigate and resolve the question marks.

The 1980s brought a somewhat weakened world economy, accompanied by high energy prices, global competition, and the rise of high-technology industries that began to supersede old economy manufacturers. In response, many companies employed the strategies of downsizing, reengineering,[2] and a quality focus. Emphasis was on efficiency and core competencies to improve profits and increase productivity. While these concepts did make business conscious of the need to reduce costs, little was attained in developing distinguishing competitive advantages to differentiate companies and their products from those of competitors.

Recent Trends in Strategic Planning

The 1990s brought a return to strategic planning, but with a focus on the involvement of line and staff managers of varying disciplines. To accompany this change in attitude, recent vision and strategic planning theories use a variety of new buzzwords.

- *Core competencies:* the focus on those activities that constitute a competitive advantage for a business
- *Coevolution or business ecosystem:* the concept of strategic alliances with customers, suppliers, and even competitors
- *Value migration:* the movement of business opportunities among industries and companies
- *Strategic intent:* a "stretch" business goal or destiny
- *White-space opportunities:* areas of growth that fall between the responsibilities of established organizational units because there is no skill or responsibility match

While these concepts are making a new generation of consultants wealthy, there is only limited evidence of consistent planning success for the businesses that pay for the reports and attempt to apply the recommendations. In one recent example discussed in the Introduction, strategic planners envisioned a telecommunications industry where integrated companies like AT&T would deliver every telecom service, including local and long distance, to traditional wireline, wireless, Internet, and cable television customers. The rush to integrate and acquire these businesses resulted in merger and acquisition activity of over $1.5 trillion in the 1996 to 2000 period.

However, the premise that bundling these services was necessary to seize market share has proven to be expensive, inflexible, and wrong. Instead, smaller, more responsive carriers likely will succeed, and AT&T and its competitors are looking for relief through global mergers, spinoffs of noncore businesses (i.e., the Lucent Technologies equipment business, formerly part of AT&T), and extensive cost cutting. Planning that allowed AT&T to increase its debt from $7 billion in 1998 to $57 billion by 2000 has left the company struggling to regain the confidence of the financial community.

Part of the reason that strategic planning often fails is that it uses existing relationships, paradigms, or thought processes. As the result, creativity and the "aha" moment of insight tend to be ignored. What has worked (i.e., a cash cow) is continued; what doesn't exist isn't invented; what hasn't yet been applied to this precise situation isn't considered.

Private and Public Sector Failures

One of hundreds of examples of business strategic planning failures[3] was the decline of Sears Roebuck as a retailing giant despite years of strategic planning studies. Sears watched Wal-Mart, Home Depot, and other retailing innovators claim many of its previously loyal customers without a meaningful reaction. The stock market value generation from 1985 to 1994 for Wal-Mart was $42 billion; for Home Depot, $20 billion; and for Sears, less than $1 billion. In the public sector a tragic example was the Vietnam War, despite the efforts of *The Best and The Brightest* minds.[4]

These failures have caused strategic planning to come into some disrepute, as it has finally been recognized that planners and consultants cannot create a strategy for a company. They can only collect data, formulate hypotheses based on that data, turn the data into information, and test their ideas using standard research methods. Planners cannot generate that spark of insight involving the necessary encyclopedic knowledge of a business, an industry, technology, and customers to concoct the next success.

If strategic planning has failed, why have seemingly intelligent businesspeople paid large sums to consultants or their internal planning staffs? One possible reason is that planning allows a company to gather intelligence about itself, to regain a semblance of control over an organization seemingly out of control. Due to economies-of-scale requirements, the modern corporation is so large and geographically dispersed that senior management often has no clue as to what its middle managers are doing[5] and whether they are pursuing the vision/business strategy. Strategic planning helps to establish a control process to derive intelligence about a company's activities.

WHAT IS CAPITAL BUDGETING?

Traditional capital budgeting supports strategic planning procedures to determine the financial viability of specific investment projects. Just as strategic planning has evolved through various phases, capital budgeting has changed from the simplistic technique of payback to the modern techniques of net present value and internal rate of return.

Payback

The payback method simply estimates the cash inflows resulting from an investment and calculates the number of years necessary to recover the total cash outlay. Opponents of this approach have two criticisms:

1. The timing of flows is ignored. For example, alternative projects costing $1,000 could have the flows listed in Exhibit 7.1. Project A has a payback of two and one-third years, while

EXHIBIT 7.1   Payback of Alternative Projects

Year	Project A	Project B
1	$500	$0
2	$400	$100
3	$300	$200
4	$200	$300
5	$100	$400
6	$0	$500
7	$0	$600
8	$0	$700
Total of Cash Flows	$1,500	$2,800

Project B has a payback at the end of year 4. We take no account of the flows in years after the payback. If we use payback, we would choose Project A; if we were to consider the total inflows from each project, we would choose Project B.

2. The payback period is not a standard measure in that it cannot be compared to any meaningful benchmark or threshold. Is a three-year payback acceptable or unacceptable? The answer would depend on the company, the year in which the decision is being made, investment alternatives, and other factors that are difficult to define.

NET PRESENT VALUE AND INTERNAL RATE OF RETURN

Net present value and internal rate of return supposedly overcome these problems by valuing each flow based on the predicted time of its occurrence and by providing a benchmark against which the calculation can be meaningfully compared. Let us review how these improvements occur.

Timing of Flows

Continuing the example developed in Exhibit 7.1, we can apply NPV and IRR to value the flows for each year in the life of an investment (see Exhibit 7.2).

EXHIBIT 7.2   Net Present Values of Alternative Projects

Year	Interest Factor	Project A*	Present Value of Flows	Project B*	Present Value of Flows
0	1.000	−$1,000	−$1,000	−$1,000	−$1,000
1	.893	$500	$447	$0	$0
2	.797	$400	$319	$100	$80
3	.712	$300	$214	$200	$142
4	.636	$200	$127	$300	$191
5	.567	$100	$57	$400	$227
6	.507	$0	$0	$500	$254
7	.452	$0	$0	$600	$271
8	.404	$0	$0	$700	$283
Totals			$164		$448

*Capital investment or "outflow" if shown as a negative number; receipts or "inflow" if shown as a positive number.
Interest Factor = present value interest factors used in calculating net present value of flows, provided in any standard tables of present and future values.

However, we have to make an assumption about the CoC (or interest rate) that is used to determine the present value of future cash inflows. For illustrative purposes, we'll use 12 percent. The results clearly show Project B with the higher NPV, but any project with a positive NPV could be chosen.

If we were to use IRR, we would be determining that interest rate which equates the outflows and inflows of cash. The IRR for level future cash flows can be determined by dividing the outflow by the annual inflow and finding the resulting interest factor in a present value of an annuity table. Since our example has uneven flows, we use a calculator to make the computation. The results are 20.3 percent for Project A and 19.7 percent for Project B.

We find that the IRRs of both projects exceed the cost of capital (assumed to be 12 percent) and would conclude that both should be selected. However, the difference between the projects is much closer using IRR than NPV. Project A has an

EXHIBIT 7.3   Conditions Causing Differing Results between NPV and IRR[a]

Characteristics of Capital Projects
■ Decreasing cash flows for Project A and increasing cash flows for Project B
■ Differing lives for each project
■ Varying costs (cash outflows) for each project

Characteristics of Corporation
■ Likely differing future returns from capital investments compared to current year returns
■ Varying future costs of capital from current year costs
■ Capital rationing, or limitations on capital available for investment

[a]Assumes two investment alternatives, Projects A and B.

IRR 3 percent higher than that of Project B, while B has an NPV which is 2.75 times that of A. If we were forced to choose, how could we explain our decision to senior management?

The answer is that each technique has different expectations about how cash inflows will be reinvested: NPV assumes the CoC rate, while IRR assumes the IRR rate. In fact, several factors can cause different results using NPV and IRR (see Exhibit 7.3). These are important differences because the IRR can be considerably higher than the CoC; recall that in our example, the CoC was 12 percent while the two IRRs were about 20 percent. Your management may well wonder if future cash flows from Project A or B can realistically be invested at 20 percent.

COST OF CAPITAL AND CASH FLOW ASSUMPTIONS

While you are pondering this problem, let's consider some other capital budgeting issues. You may recall that NPV and IRR require some assumptions as to the CoC or interest rate and expectations as to cash outflows (representing the cost of the investment) and inflows (or the income stream from that investment).

Cost-of-Capital Assumptions

Any capital budgeting looks to future returns or flows of cash, not to past successes or mistakes. For the purposes of determining the value of these flows, the CoC is calculated from the after-tax cost of debt capital and the cost of equity capital, weighted by the portion each represents in total on the balance sheet. Opinion varies as to whether short-term debt should be included. As the only short-term debt carrying a cost are notes payable and any bonds maturing within one year, it is often convenient to ignore short-term obligations in this discussion.

In lesson 5 we developed a cost of capital based on a balance sheet comprised one-third of debt and two-thirds of equity capital. We could assume the continuation of these proportions as we raise new capital, the cost of which is the CoC. Realistically, we would not raise chunks of debt and equity at the same time; however, we could attempt to maintain this relationship between debt and equity as the structure of the balance sheet is defined.

The real problem relates to the assumed costs of each new chunk of debt or equity. Capital markets are volatile, and the bonds and stocks can fluctuate 20 percent or more in a one-year period. While the causes of such variations are somewhat a matter of speculation, factors known to affect the markets include earnings expectations, the behavior of interest rates (often as influenced by Federal Reserve actions), macroeconomic trends, and global currency relationships.

Predicting the Cost of Capital

It is nearly impossible for a CFO to predict his or her company's cost of new debt or equity capital beyond the coming month or so, or even if investors will buy the securities being issued or if a lender will provide financing. These factors are extremely important in making capital budgeting decisions for two reasons, one obvious and one subtle.

1. The obvious reason is that the cost of financing any capital project cannot be known with certainty, particularly as

an investment often involves extended periods of time and costs that originally were unforeseen.

2. The subtle reason is embedded in the various assumptions regarding the use of future cash inflows (discussed in the previous section): NPV assumes reinvestment at the CoC rate, while IRR assumes the IRR rate. Since we cannot know the CoC with certainty beyond the next month or so, we can have only limited confidence in our NPV calculation. And since the IRR rate bears no relationship to the CoC rate—it is merely the mathematical result of a present value of an annuity calculation—we can have no confidence in the likelihood of the IRR result being realized.

Cash Flow Assumptions

NPV and IRR require estimations of specific costs (costs to acquire or build a capital asset, or outflows) and income (revenues less expenses, or inflows) by the period each will be incurred. However, how do we ever know what a project costs in total or when those costs will be incurred until all of the relevant expenses are tabulated? And how can we predict future income streams before an investment is made? It is often a matter of conjecture whether we will ever receive a return from a capital project.

Take another look at Exhibit 7.1. Will Project A really throw off $500 in the first year after the investment and positive flows in the succeeding four years? Will Project B show increasing flows after the first year? How can anyone predict cash flows out to years 6 through 8? Experienced CFOs know that such predictions are fanciful and that forecasts are based on what is known today and then extrapolated into the future.

ADJUSTING FOR CAPITAL BUDGETING RISK

Economists often use probabilities to evaluate uncertainty, and finance has adapted these techniques to cash flow analysis.

Decision Making under Uncertainty

The uncertainty of a future flow can be evaluated by assigned probabilities to various possible outcomes. For example, the

EXHIBIT 7.4   Expected Present Values for Year 2 Inflows

Cash Inflow Forecast	Probability	Outcome	Expected Value
Project A			
Below Forecast	.30	$300	$90
Meets Forecast	.50	$400	$200
Exceeds Forecast	.20	$500	$100
Expected Value	1.00		$390
PV of Expected Value[a]			$311
Project B			
Below Forecast	.35	$0	$0
Meets Forecast	.45	$100	$45
Exceeds Forecast	.20	$200	$40
Expected Value	1.00		$85
PV of Expected Value[a]			$68

[a]Present Value of Year 2 at a 12 percent interest rate = .797.

$500 from Project A in year 1 actually may be as little as $300 or as much as $700, with $500 only our best guess as to the result. If we assign probabilities to possible results, we can develop expected values for each future year. In Exhibit 7.4, probabilities are assigned to year 2's results for Projects A and B.

Similarly, each year's flows could be assigned probabilities, and a total expected value for the two projects could be determined. The problem with this approach is that probabilities are entirely hypothetical. We have no knowledge of the likelihood of any particular outcome, and, by their very nature, most capital projects usually have no historical record from which probabilities can be extrapolated.

An alternative approach is to assign a risk-adjusted CoC in the valuation of each capital alternative. The difference between the risk-adjusted rate and the return on a riskless asset (such as a 91-day U.S. Treasury Bill) is known as the risk premium, and the risk is measured by a statistic known as the coefficient of variation (v). The coefficient of variation is defined as the standard deviation of a distribution (σ) divided by the expected or mean value. This approach is scientifically appealing but requires judgment both as to the risk premium and to the magnitude of the statistic. If utilized, it would require a separate CoC for each investment option.

Real-Options Analysis

The unpredictability of capital budgeting outcomes has led to attempts to go beyond probabilities and risk-adjusted CoCs. Unlike NPV and IRR, real-options analysis allows companies to develop various alternatives to each investment and to implement those alternatives determined appropriate as future conditions are encountered. Real options is derived from the options theory embedded in the Black-Scholes model that is used in the options markets and in valuing derivatives.[6]

In one application, a rise in energy prices and/or shortages would cause relatively inefficient gas-fired power plants temporarily to generate electricity as required to satisfy the spot market. As prices fall and/or shortages disappear, these plants can be shut down. Hewlett-Packard and Anadarko Petroleum are among several companies that have successfully utilized this technique.[7] The development of various capital projects and then the implementation of the appropriate project at the opportune time allow for greater flexibility and responsiveness to changing market conditions.

Capital Budgeting Anxiety

Capital budgets tend to follow forecasts of economic activity in a herdlike pattern, as companies jump into or out of investments based on their access to capital and their perceptions of general business conditions. For example, in 2001 capital spending was down by about 1.5 percent annualized after several years of significant expansion. With tepid stock and bond markets, the external financing required to fund capital projects was no longer readily available.

The telecommunications industry is a classic example of capital investing responding to unrealistic hype and hope. When the entire industry, along with investors, analysts, and lenders, determined that revenue and profit forecasts could not be attained, stock prices dropped, forcing the industry to reduce operating and capital budgets.

This is not the way business is supposed to work, yet the telecommunications situation reflects the heart of the problem with strategic planning and capital budgeting. The uncertainty over nearly every facet of an investment decision, from demand through pricing, the actions of competitors, the CoC, effects of competitive technologies, and the response of regulators, makes the process nearly futile.

CONCLUSIONS

The role of the CFO is to oversee the process of strategic planning and its financial element, capital budgeting, to make certain that the logic and method in strategic planning is understood as a package of questionable conclusions about the future. Flexibility through real-options analysis or similar processes is necessary to ensure corporate survival. Quantitative certainty in NPV and IRR or other techniques should be appreciated as attractive illusions that may or may not come to pass.

NOTES

1. Theodore Levitt, "Marketing Myopia," *Harvard Business Review,* Vol. 38, July/August 1960, pp. 45–56.
2. For financial implications of reengineering, see James Sagner, *Cashflow Reengineering* (New York: AMACOM Books, 1997).
3. See the definitive review of the subject by Henry Mintzberg, *The Rise and Fall of Strategic Planning* (New York: The Free Press, 1994).
4. To use the title of David Halberstam's landmark history, *The Best and the Brightest* (New York: Random House, 1972).
5. See the discussion in James Sagner, *Investing in the New Economy* (New York: Wiley/Fabozzi, 2001), chapter 4.
6. The Black-Scholes model is based on the work of Myron Scholes, Robert Merton, and Fischer Black on the valuation of options. For their work, Scholes and Merton won the Nobel Prize in Economics in 1997.
7. See "Exploiting Uncertainty," *Business Week,* June 7, 1999, pp. 118–122.

Rating Agencies

What they taught in your MBA finance program:

Rating agencies provide objective evaluations to lenders, creditors, and investors of the financial position of the corporation under review.

What they should have taught:

Rating agencies have developed a significant investment community role due to their status as nationally recognized statistical rating organizations. This position has led to various problems with ratings, including accuracy, objectivity, coercive tactics, and questionable credentialing, problems that so far have been ignored by the regulators.

ROLE OF THE RATING AGENCIES

The purpose of rating agency evaluations is to provide objective analysis of the creditworthiness of a corporation. However, ratings have become a negotiation between raters and companies, with raters looking at strategies, management, and other qualitative factors, not just financial measures. Raters often lack industry experience, and companies that search out "friendly raters" may receive higher marks than are warranted.

The work of credit rating agencies has evolved into a critical function in our financial system, yet there is little information generally available on who they are and what they do. Most finance courses do not discuss these activities, and few texts provide any more than a cursory comment.[1] Furthermore, while access to capital is available from a wide array of lenders and investors, credit ratings are established by a small group of entrenched raters using confidential procedures.

Despite the fact that issuers pay for the rating, the raters represent investors and lenders, not issuers. Certain rating agencies have been known to pressure companies to purchase ancillary services, and this selling orientation may be leading to less than totally objective results. While ratings often are issued at the request of the issuer, occasionally they are issued and invoiced on an unsolicited basis.

Who Are the Raters?

As a current or future issuer of or investor in short- and longer-term securities, your organization will encounter rating agencies as you attempt to go to market or place investable funds. You should know who they are and what they do. Three major rating agencies provide general credit analysis of corporate and governmental financial instruments (see Exhibit 8.1).

EXHIBIT 8.1   Major Credit Rating Agencies

Rating Agency and Short Name	Parent	Market Scope	Ratings Scales[a]
Moody's Investor Services (Moody's)	Dun and Bradstreet; a separate company since 2000	Global	CP: P-1 through P-3 L-T: Aaa through C
Standard & Poor's (S&P)	McGraw-Hill	Global	CP: A-1+ through D L-T: AAA through D
Fitch	Fimalac-Euronotation-IBCA-Fitch-Duff & Phelps	Primarily Europe with U.S. presence	CP: A1+ through D1 L-T: AAA through C

[a]CP: ratings for commercial paper and short-term securities. L-T: ratings for long-term securities (beyond one year in maturity).

Specialized raters deal with specific industries. For example, A.M. Best rates insurance companies writing life and health, and property and casualty coverage; Thomson Bank Watch and Lace Financial review bank creditworthiness; and Capital Intelligence Ltd. provides analysis of companies primarily domiciled in the Middle East, North Africa, and other developing areas of the globe.

What Raters Do

We'll review the analytical process used by these agencies in the next section. In brief, the ratings process involves the review of public documents, such as annual reports and 10-K filings with the Securities and Exchange Commission; and confidential company documents, including business plans, costing studies, accounting reports, and customer profitability analyses. These data are explained and supplemented by discussions with management on recent performance and future strategies.

The evaluations result in credit ratings for specific debt issues based on the issuer's ability to repay interest and principal. This is different from the earnings perspective of equity analysts, who calculate earnings per share; returns on assets, equity, or sales; the price/earnings ratio; or market capitalization. Although assignments vary by rating agency, the general approach to the assignment of ratings is as follows:

- Repayment on time usually is given one of the investment-grade ratings (AAA to A).
- The possibility of not being paid on time is considered noninvestment grade (BBB to B).
- The possibility of not being paid in full is known colloquially as junk (C).
- The fact of not paying is considered as in default (D).

The ratings drive the cost that the issuer will pay for funds and even access to funds at any price: An A rating (single through triple A) will result in significantly lower costs and higher market acceptance than ratings in the Bs (or lower). See

EXHIBIT 8.2 Recent Spreads between Bond Rate Classes

Year	Aaa (%)	Aa (%)	A (%)	Baa (%)
1995	7.41	7.54	7.65	8.04
1996	7.65	7.82	7.97	8.35
1997	7.14	7.36	7.42	7.75
1998	6.55	6.78	6.89	7.15
1999	7.19	7.48	7.65	7.95
2000	7.65	7.81	8.11	8.35
Average Yield[a]	7.27	7.47	7.62	7.93
Incremental Yield Required		0.20	0.35	0.66

Source: Moody's Bond Record, December 2000, p. 54.
[a]Yields are for corporate bonds issued in midyear.

Exhibit 8.2 for the recent nominal and incremental spreads between various grades of debt classes.

The additional interest cost for a hypothetical 20-year, $25 million issue is as follows:

Aa rating rather than Aaa rating: $1.0 million
A rating rather than AA rating: $0.75 million
Baa rating rather than A rating: $1.5 million

These amounts are based on simple interest calculations, that is, without considering the time value of money of the additional interest paid.

The "premium" that the markets require for lower-rated instruments will vary over time, usually from the supply-and-demand situation for funds and from market attitude toward the acceptance or avoidance of risk. Risk is less palatable in an economic slowdown or during geopolitical stress than in an expansion and relative peaceful conditions. Issuers may be forced to pay a greater premium for funds in recessionary times or when there are world or regional crises.

Costs

There is very little public information on the fees charged by credit rating agencies. An irony of the credit ratings business is that charges are assessed on the borrowing entity, but the value is primarily to the lending organization. It is known that many Fortune 500–size borrowers pay as much as $100,000 or more per year, with smaller companies charged in the annual low to mid-five figures.

HOW RATINGS ARE CONSTRUCTED

The precise process in developing a rating is confidential, although the analysis is known to focus on industry comparisons, financial performance and stability, and the quality of management. The ratings agencies do not use a formula or standard template but review each company with due respect for unusual factors, trends and developments, and various nonquantifiable concerns.

Industry Analysis

In conducting an industry analysis, raters examine the structure and stability of the industry, including barriers to entry, global competition, the maturity or position in the industry's cycle, and capital requirements for technology, plant and equipment, research and development, and employee expertise. Industry analysis beginning in the 1920s developed the significant ratio approach, which compares various balance-sheet and income statement entries.

Ratios are published for liquidity or solvency, activity or efficiency, and profitability by Dun & Bradstreet and the Risk Management Association (or RMA, formerly Robert Morris Associates). The objective is to determine if a company's performance is outside the normal (or interquartile) range. (There are four quartiles in any array, equivalent to the 25th, 50th, 75th, and 100th percentiles. The interquartile range is between the

25th percentile or 1st quartile and 75th percentile or 3rd quartile.) However, aggressive management may deliberately run down balance-sheet accounts to reduce "unproductive" assets and increase operating and financial leverage.[2] Recall the discussion of Dell Computer in lesson 2: as shown in Exhibit 8.3, Dell falls outside of the normal range for several of the significant ratios, shown underlined.

The performance of the four outlying ratios is directly traceable to the Dell philosophy of minimal receivables, just-in-time delivery of inventory, little need for debt financing, and high sales turnover. However, inexperienced ratings analysts might assume that the company is underperforming the industry and assign a lower rating than is warranted by performance over time.

EXHIBIT 8.3 Significant Ratios for the Computer Industry and for Dell Computer

Industry Data	3rd Quartile	Median	1st Quartile	Dell Computer
Current Ratio	2.1	1.6	1.1	1.4
Quick Ratio	1.6	0.9	0.6	1.2
Sales/Receivables	10.0	5.6	4.4	11.0[a]
CGS[b]/Inventory	12.4	5.4	4.0	63.6
CGS/Payables	11.9	9.3	5.9	5.9
Sales/Working Capital	4.0	10.3	35.6	10.8
EBIT[c]/Interest	19.6	9.0	−8.1	−6.0
Fixed Assets/Net Worth	0.2	0.4	0.9	0.2
Debt/Net Worth	0.6	1.7	3.7	0.2
Sales/Fixed Assets	34.5	17.3	5.1	32.0
Sales/Assets	2.3	1.4	1.0	2.4

Sources: Significant ratios are from Risk Management Association, *Annual Statement Studies, 2000–2001,* SIC 3571, p. 559. Dell Computer statistics are calculated from the annual report for the fiscal year ending January 2001.

[a]Underlined results for Dell lie outside of the "normal range" of industry ratios.

[b]CGS = cost of goods sold.

[c]EBIT = earnings before income taxes.

Financial Performance and Stability

There are several components to financial results and fiscal stability, including accounting quality, cash flow, earnings, and the capital structure. Raters, of course, do not audit financial statements, but they do review statement construction based on the company's accounting policies, the treatment of specific classes of accounts (e.g., goodwill, depreciation, inventory), and the content of off–balance-sheet items and notes to the statements.

Cash flow and earnings are critical to a company's capacity to service its debt (including interest and principal payments) and to finance current and future business operations. Cash flow projections are analyzed to determine if projected flows are reasonable in the context of recent performance. Capital structure issues include the degree of financial leverage (the ratio of debt to equity), which drives the cost of capital and the likelihood of raising additional long-term financing.

Quality of Management

The subjective nature of the assessment of management makes the relationship between the rating agency and the company a primary concern. CFOs (and chief executive officers, or CEOs) spend considerable effort to "court" the raters through presentations, discussions, and interviews. Rating analysts supplement these impressions with the comparison of performance against stated goals over time. Consideration is given to length of tenure in senior positions, turnover, industry and general business experience, and succession planning.

Meetings are held between rating agencies and issuers to establish the company's ratings goals. Once these goals are set and communicated, the rating agency monitors performance and notifies the company should there be a problem. Similarly, the company can inform the agency when adverse developments occur to mitigate any negative impact and to show management's responsiveness to changing business conditions.

RATING AGENCY PROBLEMS

In effect, the rating agencies are market regulators without any official status or qualification requirement. They benefit from practices that could be considered as abusive, in that their opinions are absolute, derived from complex and confidential reviews, and not subject to either minimal professional standards or peer review. An examination of various legal pleadings and other public documents indicates the following problems.

Accuracy Issues

The accuracy of the raters in evaluating creditworthiness and risk of rated organizations has been tested by the error situation described in the Introduction and by the disclosure of derivative losses of various companies (i.e., Procter & Gamble) and not-for-profit organizations (i.e., Orange County, California). These events certainly reflect an absence of a sense of fiduciary responsibility and oversight by company boards of directors and by Orange County's board of supervisors.

Where were the rating agencies, and why were no steps taken to review exposures to financial risks? Similarly, missed revenue and profit forecasts, overinvestment in capital equipment or business acquisitions, and corporate failures have occurred without adequate warnings by the rating agencies.

Objectivity Issues

The issue of objectivity reflects the orientation of the agencies and depends on whether the reference is to the older, established raters (Moody's and Standard & Poor's) or the newer, less established firms. Fitch is clearly attempting to build acceptance and position and will take no actions that impede that strategy.

These concerns are particularly important, as any increase in market share by one agency must inevitably come at the expense of the others; after all, no issuer requires three sets of independent ratings. The competition for market share has led to "rate surfing" by issuers, which involves shopping among the agencies and rejecting unfavorable ratings.

Coercion Issues

The competition between the rating agencies has led to the disputed practice of providing unsolicited ratings, that is, the evaluation of new issues without being contracted to do the rating and without access to internal information about the issuer. Furthermore, Moody's has been known to invoice and pressure for payment for its services whether the company had been hired or not.

When Moody's is not selected to review a company's new issue, it has withdrawn ratings on all other issues, an action that, to the markets, implies a credit rating downgrade. Many issuers resent Moody's tactics, and the entire investment community fears that credit ratings could be colored by undue rating agency pressure. There have been reports of threats by rating agencies regarding future ratings downgrades, although these appear to have ended some years ago.

Because of Moody's potentially coercive power, the Justice Department's Antitrust Division began an investigation in 1996 of possible intimidation in forcing issuers to use the various credit rating services. Various market participants, including investment bankers and debt issuers, told investigators about Moody's supposedly coercive tactics in obtaining business. The inquiry was concluded in early 1999 with no action being taken by the government. However, various changes occurred within the Moody's organization during this period, possibly reflecting the government's concerns.

In addition, Colorado and California issuers (a school district and a health maintenance organization) sued rating agencies (Moody's and a small agency, the Weiss Group, respectively) for libel and defamation on the grounds of adverse market reaction to unsolicited opinions. However, these suits were dismissed, with the judges appearing to be reluctant to interfere with an ostensibly objective rating process and the free speech protections of the First Amendment.

Qualifications Issues

A recurrent criticism of the agencies is analysts' lack of experience, possibly leading to misunderstandings as to appropriate organizational practice and management. While inexperience probably occurs throughout the profession due to turnover, it may be worse at Moody's and Standard & Poor's. This perception of inexperience is particularly troubling given the current orientation to strategy and plans, requiring extensive knowledge of and experience with the industry being reviewed. In contrast, more junior analysts can conduct traditional, financial credit ratings.

Despite these problems, most companies seem to believe that their ratings are approximately correct.[3] Moody's continues to have the greatest proportion of dissatisfied clients, which is probably to be expected given the firm's long-established orientation to investors and not borrowers.

SO, WHO'S RATING THE RATING AGENCIES?

The power and impact of the rating agencies arguably exceeds the role normally accorded independent agencies or firms in a capitalistic system and effectively makes the agencies arbiters of who will have access to the debt markets and at what cost. In fact, the interactive role of the agencies in reviewing business strategies and results creates an oversight function not mandated by any U.S. regulation or statute. In order to appreciate the origin of this status, it is useful to examine recent rating agency history.[4]

Nationally Recognized Statistical Rating Organization Designation

Commercial paper has been issued during much of the 20th and all of the 21st century with few instances of default and losses to lenders. However, the 1970 bankruptcy of Penn Central surprised the credit markets, which had purchased over $80 million of the company's paper. The Securities and Exchange

Commission responded in 1975 with rule 15c3-1 governing the net capital securities firms ("broker-dealers").

The rule required the deduction of a certain percentage (or "haircut") of the market value but allowed preferential treatment to certain investments (including commercial paper) rated investment grade by two or more nationally recognized statistical rating organizations (NRSROs). As the result, NRSROs— Moody's, Standard & Poor's, and Fitch—are accorded the status of regulators by the SEC without any specific requirement for qualifications or experience, and their determinations are not subject to any appeal.

Securities and Exchange Commission Takes Another Look

Lately the SEC has become concerned with the power of the NRSROs, and in 1997 it proposed new criteria for rating agencies to receive such recognition.

- *Recognition.* The NRSRO must be recognized as a credible and reliable issuer of ratings by the users of ratings services.
- *Qualifications.* The ratings agency is required to have adequate resources to develop credible ratings independent of pressure or economic coercion from the corporations or organizations being rated. These resources must include educated and qualified staff.
- *Systematic procedures.* The procedures used must ensure the development of accurate ratings.
- *Management access.* The NRSRO must have ample contact with company management.
- *Internal compliance.* The ratings agency must have adequate internal procedures to prevent the misuse of confidential data.

Twenty-five respondents supported the concept of the NRSRO, although some comments suggested that statistical models or historical interest spreads be used to determine the risk level associated with particular securities. The SEC staff concluded that statistical analysis would be valid only where there is a "deep and liquid market for the instrument. . . . It would not be adequate for debt issuers with no previously issued or very old public debt" or where the market is illiquid.[5] As the result of the general acceptance of the NRSRO designation, the SEC has not proceeded with any new final rulemaking to change rating agency procedures.

Power of the Rating Agencies

There are three significant results of the NRSRO mandate:

1. An issuer of debt instruments must obtain a credit rating so that it can be accorded market acceptance status. Debt issuance has become a global market, particularly as the after-tax cost is one-third that of the cost of equity. Without a credit rating, it is difficult for a company to go to the public markets to obtain capital.

2. The requirement for a credit rating ensures the business position of the agencies designated as NRSROs. Furthermore, the resources dedicated to corporate credit analysis by financial institutions have declined significantly (see lesson 5). As a result, there is an even greater dependence by lenders and investors on the work of the credit rating agencies.

3. The murkiness of the criteria for recognition protects existing rating agencies from new competitors. While the SEC would not agree that aspiring NRSROs are denied entry, few companies have even bothered to qualify. Fimalac finally gained entry in 1997 through its acquisition of Fitch and Duff & Phelps.

Another reason for the power of the ratings agencies is the sheer number of companies seeking commercial paper or bond financing, particularly as institutional investors—the principal purchasers of debt securities—have restrictive ratings requirements for their investment portfolios. For example, guidelines may prohibit holding a security with a rating below A, with a

EXHIBIT 8.4   Typical Investment Policy Credit Quality Restrictions

In general, the company will only purchase and maintain high-quality
    investment securities in keeping with the primary objective of the
    Investment Policy being preservation of capital.
The credit ratings given by the nationally recognized credit rating
    agencies are to be used for determining minimum levels of acceptable
    credit quality.
For short-term investments only the highest-quality short-term rating is
    allowed. In addition, if the issuer of a short-term investment also has a
    long-term rating, that long-term rating must be A or better as explained
    next.
Long-term investments (securities whose original maturity date is beyond
    one year) require a rating of A or better.
Other quality standards, as deemed relevant by the CFO, also may be
    used to establish additional requirements for credit quality.

target weighted portfolio average between AA and A. See Exhibit 8.4 for typical investment policy language.

CONCLUSIONS

The CFO has no choice but to work closely with the rating agencies to elicit the highest possible grade for commercial paper and
bond financings. Unless and until the SEC chooses to restrain the
NRSROs, their power is so strong and their hold on the financial
markets so complete that any resistance is futile and potentially
destructively expensive. Unfortunately, even the mild proposals
regarding recognition, qualifications, systematic procedures,
management access, and internal compliance have been tabled,
and no one knows how the rating agencies really do their work,
if the raters are adequately qualified, or if coercive tactics are
used to extract cooperation and additional fee income.

     With the rating agencies now providing prospective ratings—
to address such concerns as what would happen if we did this
or that?—they are essentially becoming strategic consultants. If
their credentials are of concern regarding past performance reviews, can anyone imagine that they are qualified as advisors
to management?

Rating agency meetings to review plans and expected results are an essential part of the CFO's job. For a company to be successful with the NRSROs, the dialogue between the organization being rated and the agency should be continuous to review industry or company developments and to examine the potential credit implications of a proposed venture. Any significant business developments should be communicated to rating agencies prior to a public announcement. Presentations should be fresh and technologically sophisticated, and attended by senior management including the CFO and, if possible, the CEO.

We expect increasing competition among the rating agencies for business, with the accompanying demand for access to managers to discuss company activities. Such efforts are through the CFO's door, and he or she should be prepared with appropriate responses. Those rating agencies will expect a broad exposure to the operations of the organization. Raters will not be satisfied merely with historical financial data. They will want a comprehensive description of the business and will expect appropriate access for questions and discussion.

NOTES

1. For example, Lawrence J. Gitman, *Principles of Managerial Finance,* 9th ed. (Reading, MA: Addison-Wesley, 2000), does not mention the rating agencies in its 900+ pages, while Marcia L. Stigum's encyclopedic study *The Money Market,* 3rd ed., notes them in a brief passage in the discussion of commercial paper (p. 1038); (Homewood, IL: Dow Jones-Irwin, 1990).

2. For additional discussion of these issues, see James S. Sagner, *Investing in the New Economy* (New York: Wiley/Fabozzi, 2001), chapter 2.

3. See, for example, Joseph Cantwell, "Managing Credit Ratings and Rating Agency Relationships," *TMA Journal* (now *AFP Exchange*), November/ December 1998, pp. 14–22 at 16.

4. For a more complete discussion of these issues, see Andrew Fight, *The Ratings Game* (New York: John Wiley & Sons, 2001), particularly chapter 5.

5. SEC Proposed Rule, Release No. 34-39457, File No. S7-33-97, December 17, 1997, p. 8. The document can be accessed at *www.sec.gov/rules/ proposed/34-39457.txt.*

Investment Banking

What they taught in your MBA finance program:

> Investment bankers provide professional advice to companies on the structure of their balance sheets, how to raise debt and equity, and similar matters.

What they should have taught:

> Investment bankers are subject to the same temptations as any manager of invested capital and cannot be assumed to behave as independent professionals acting in the best interests of their clients. CFOs must diligently review, consider, and independently appraise the quality of any service offered by the investment banking community.

SECURITIES INDUSTRY ACTIVITIES

The securities industry is comprised of several diverse activities that are described in the sections that follow. The largest firms, including Merrill Lynch, Salomon Smith Barney, and Morgan Stanley Dean Witter, provide all of these services to clients. Other firms specialize in certain securities functions:

- Investment banking: for example, Goldman Sachs
- Commercial banking: for example, J. P. Morgan Chase
- Discount brokerage: for example, Charles Schwab
- Mutual funds: for example, Fidelity Investments

Investment Management

Securities firms develop a large portion of their revenue from the management of assets for themselves and for pension funds, trusts, and various institutional and private investors. Although there is substantial competition for such business, the stability and size of the potential assets make investment management a primary focus of sales activities.

Investment Banking

The underwriting and distribution of new debt and equity issues constitute the principal function of investment banking. There are various types of underwriting activities, including initial public offerings (IPOs), the first issuance of securities by a private firm, and secondary issues, the distribution of new securities by publicly traded companies. A related function—market making—involves developing and supporting a market for a specific security, to provide liquidity and stability to the markets.

Trading

Much of a securities firm's trading activity supports short-term positioning to support secondary market making. Arbitrage establishes offsetting trading positions at slightly different prices. Price differences for a security can occur when there is buying and selling in multiple markets or when differing instruments of the same group of issuers are traded, as during the period when two publicly traded companies are merging at an announced share exchange ratio.

Mergers and Acquisitions

Until the recent economic downturn, a significant source of investment banking revenue was merger and acquisition (M&A) advice or assistance.[1] Such activities include finding merger candidates; establishing valuations; and arranging for the merger agreement, including the management of the surviving company and the apportionment of cash, debt, and equity financing.

Retail Brokerage

Securities firms that offer retail brokerage services derive fees from commissions paid by customers on trading activity and from various ancillary services necessary to allow the markets to execute buy and sell orders. These services include the following:

- *Stock loan:* the lending of securities held on behalf of customers to firms requiring a security to make delivery resulting from a sale or short sale
- *Clearance and settlement:* the delivery (or proof of ownership) of securities that have been sold and the receipt of funds in settlement of the trade
- *Margin interest:* a loan to the securities buyer of a portion of the cost of a transaction at an interest cost often below a bank's loan rate

PARTNERSHIP STRUCTURES

Investment banking was a European institution going back several centuries, with the largest banking houses supporting both commercial and national enterprises by loans and the sale of securities. Governments often required infusions of cash to fight wars, such as the Crimean War, or build great public works, such as the Suez Canal, both of which were financed in part by the leading investment banking firm, the House of Rothschild.[2] The longevity of European banking houses was made possible by European monarchy and succession, and the close relationships that developed among the royal courts, their governments, and the bankers endured, in some instances, for centuries.

Founding U.S. Investment Bankers

Those concepts were brought to the United States by such early investment bankers as Jay Cooke, August Belmont, and J. P. Morgan. Cooke played an important role in financing the Union Army during the Civil War, when the U.S. government had only limited capabilities to issue debt and tax. Belmont, originally the Rothschild representative in the United States, quickly became an important New York investment banker. He supported the country's financing requirements during the Mexican and Civil Wars and assisted in funding numerous state and municipal projects.

J. Pierpont Morgan is probably the best known of all of the founding investment banking figures. Morgan organized railroad ventures and created U.S. Steel after buying Carnegie Steel from Andrew Carnegie for $400 million. However, his most important economic contribution undoubtedly was leading a group of bankers in stopping the Panic of 1907 in a "private" rescue. As the result of the 1907 incident and several earlier panics, Congress passed the Federal Reserve Act of 1913 to create a central bank that could act as lender of last resort.

Partnership Honor and Trust

As practiced by the early firms, investment banking was a partnership business. Partnership was an appropriate form of ownership to represent the strong, honorable leader and was appropriate due to the relatively short life of most investment banking deals. However, the partnership ownership form is always a disadvantage in ensuring continuity and in accumulating sufficient equity capital for a growing U.S. and later global economy.

Continuity is a problem as partners retire or die and their capital contribution is withdrawn from the firm. In the United States (unlike Europe), continuity can be affected by changes in the leadership of the national or state government. Capital adequacy is also a concern, as any funds raised on behalf of clients would depend on the size of the equity base supporting borrowing and/or the sale of debt instruments.

Most early investment bankers generally subscribed to the principle that honor and trust were essential attributes of the investment banker. Many interrupted careers to serve in government, and several were U.S. Treasury secretaries. Morgan's words on this point are revealing. When asked if credit was granted based on solvency, he replied: "No, Sir. It is because people believe in the man. . . . A man I do not trust could not get money from me on all the bonds in Christendom."[3]

Nineteenth-Century Dishonor

Scoundrels were present on Wall Street almost from the beginning. Jay Gould and Jim Fisk attempted to corner the gold market in 1869, leading to a significant economic panic. The Crédit Mobilier scandal of the 1870s involved bribes to members of Congress by railroad executives. A conflict arose between certain of the principals, leading to a governmental investigation.

Even former president and Civil War general Ulysses S. Grant was defrauded and his brokerage firm destroyed by his partner, Ferdinand Ward, who embezzled more than $2 million from the firm in 1884. However, these and other episodes did not result in any regulatory initiatives or governmental action, as they were considered to be isolated events.

PUBLIC POLICY TOWARD THE SECURITIES INDUSTRY

Like commercial banking, discussed in lessons 5 and 6, the securities industry is special because of the fiduciary (or trust) nature of the relationship the industry has with its clients. That is, these financial institutions hold or raise funds on behalf of businesses (and consumers) and provide advice for a fee on the most appropriate manner to accomplish these services. This dependency on client trust in their financial advisors was originally thought to be a matter of honor, although by the twentieth century it had become a matter of law. Why did public policy toward investment banking change so completely?

Securities Legislation

The stock market crash in October 1929 largely ended any illusions regarding the unquestioned integrity of the investment banks. During the Pecora hearings on the causes of the crash early in the first Franklin Roosevelt administration, evidence of various irregularities in the markets was established. These "irregularities" included fixed fees rather than competitive bidding for new issues, the "parking" of stock in commercial bank trust departments, the excesses and lack of accountability of investment trusts, and numerous other actions generally held to be against public policy.

Undeniably searching for a scapegoat for the Great Depression, Congress demanded adequate regulatory supervision of the markets. The Securities Act of 1933 required full financial disclosure and the registration of newly issued securities. Created by the Securities Exchange Act of 1934, regulatory and registration functions were assigned to the Securities and Exchange Commission a year later. The securities industry also depends on self-regulation (through the New York Stock Exchange and the National Association of Securities Dealers) to monitor trading abuses and the capital adequacy of securities firms. The Glass-Stegall Act of 1933, requiring the separation of commercial and investment banking, was not repealed until 1999 (see lesson 5). The results of this legislative oversight included basic changes in the traditional conduct of the investment banking business. For firms like J. P. Morgan—which became Morgan Stanley for investment banking and Morgan Guaranty (later J. P. Morgan Chase) for commercial banking—these severe restrictions resulted in limitations on access to the capital required for financings.

Aftermath

Although generally furious with the interference of Congress, the securities industry had little choice but to change its behavior in accordance with the new regulations. However, business actually was impacted only slightly for the next decade, largely because there was little business to do. Civilian economic activity was suppressed until after World War II. There was very little demand for private investment financing during the 1930s, and much of the 1940s were spent in massive government programs in support of the war effort, in war relief, and in conversion to peacetime activities.

MAIN STREET BROKERS

The prosperity of the 1920s began to change the orientation of the securities firms from investment banking to the distribution of bonds and equities through branch offices. Underwriting provided attractive revenues, but the retail and institutional clamor for investment products and the need to market new securities issues signaled a major change in the industry's focus. Local offices were established in cities and towns, connected to the New York City home office by telex and telephone, and the firms that developed this system became known as wire houses.

Wire Houses

Retail clients began to seek the services of investment advisors when Liberty Loan bonds from World War I started to mature in the mid-1920's. The subsequent American economic boom drew many new, unsophisticated participants. Merrill Lynch epitomized the wire house firm, offering a trustworthy sales force, supported by training, research, institutional advertising, and negative as well as positive economic forecasts. To its credit, Merrill Lynch realized the problems facing the stock market by early 1928 and advocated that its customers reduce their stock positions. Other firms that generally followed this model included E. F. Hutton, Paine Webber Jackson & Curtis, Dean Witter, and Bear Stearns.

Post–World War II Boom

Financial services changed dramatically following World War II, reflecting the creation and promotion of new investment vehicles and the perception of commercial banking as stodgy. Individual and later institutional investors flocked to mutual funds as discretionary investments and were pleased to see their employers contributing to pension funds and other retirement plans. Exhibit 9.1 shows the decline of bank and thrift assets in favor of newer types of investments favoring equity assets.

EXHIBIT 9.1 Asset Shares in Various Financial Investments (%)

	1912	1922	1929	1939	1948	1960	1970	1980	1997
Commercial Banks	64.5	63.3	53.7	51.2	55.9	38.2	37.9	34.8	36.1
Thrifts	14.8	13.9	14.0	13.6	12.3	19.7	20.4	21.4	10.8
BANKS/THRIFTS	79.3	77.2	67.7	64.8	68.2	57.9	58.3	56.2	46.9
Insurance Companies	16.6	16.7	18.6	27.2	24.3	23.8	18.9	16.1	19.3
Securities Firms	3.0	5.3	8.1	1.5	1.0	1.1	1.2	1.1	1.5
Mutual Funds	0.0	0.0	2.4	1.9	1.3	2.9	3.5	3.6	14.3
Pension Funds	0.0	0.0	0.7	2.1	3.1	9.7	13.0	17.4	11.6
INVESTMENT BANKERS	3.0	5.3	11.2	5.5	5.4	13.7	17.7	22.1	27.4
FINANCE COMPANIES	0.0	0.0	2.0	2.2	2.0	4.6	4.8	5.1	5.9
OTHER	1.1	0.8	0.5	0.3	0.1	0.0	0.3	0.5	0.5

Source: Developed from material in Anthony Saunders, *Financial Institutions Management*, 3rd ed. (New York: McGraw-Hill, 2000), p. 98 (Table 6.3).

However, these statistics are somewhat misleading, as the banks actively participate in the settlement of securities, hold a substantial portion as fiduciaries, and conduct extensive off–balance sheet activities.[4] Off–balance sheet activities consist of contingent transactions that have the potential—if exercised—to affect bank cash flow and profitability. By one estimate, off–balance sheet commitments totaled nearly $30 trillion by the end of the twentieth century. The largest such activities include interest rate swaps, loan and foreign exchange commitments, and futures contracts.

At the same time, long-repressed consumer demand, funded by wartime income held as savings accounts or bonds, fueled a resurgent global economy. The resulting requirement for capital strained the resources of the investment banking partnerships. Over the next two decades, these firms were forced to convert their form of ownership to that of publicly traded corporations in order to develop sufficient capital to meet the soaring capital demands of their industrial and financial clients. Exhibit 9.2 lists significant changes of ownership structure for large securities firms.

Other Problems Emerge

In addition to investment bank capital constraints, the securities industry faced various problems in the decades following World War II.

Securities Clearing and Settlement. Prior to the advent of computers, all securities transactions had to be cleared and settled by the hand delivery of certificates and the transfer of funds. An extensive investment in clerical staff and systems was required to convert to the electronic matching of trades, and hundreds of firms were unable to make the necessary commitment of funds. In contrast, most transactions today are book entry, eliminating the requirement for the physical delivery and reissue of stock or bond certificates. The extent of the problem became apparent in the late 1960s, with the largest failures being Goodbody & Co. and F. I. duPont & Co.

EXHIBIT 9.2 Investment Banker Ownership Structure Changes

1971:	Merrill Lynch becomes a public company.
1972:	E. F. Hutton becomes a public company.
1981:	Salomon Bros. merges with Phibro; again becomes private in 1985.
1985:	Kidder Peabody sold to General Electric (80 percent share); resold to Paine Webber in 1995.
1986:	Morgan Stanley becomes a public company.
1986:	Dillon Read sold to Travelers Insurance; portions resold to Baring Bros. (U.K.); then again becomes a private company.
1987:	Shearson acquires E. F. Hutton.
1987:	Shearson American Express acquires Lehman Bros.; again becomes private in 1994.
1997:	Bankers Trust acquires Alex. Brown & Sons; currently a unit of Deutsche Bank.
1997:	Dillon Reed sold to Swiss Bank Corp. (as Warburg Dillion Reed).
1997:	Travelers Insurance (now Citigroup) acquires Salomon Bros. and merges it into Smith Barney.
1999:	Goldman Sachs becomes a public company.

Source: Derived from Charles R. Geisst, *The Last Partnerships* (New York: McGraw-Hill, 2001); supplemented by data in the websites of the surviving firms.

Globalization. The world's securities markets have expedited the settlement of securities transactions through standardization and systematic reductions in clearing times.[5] Market participants are becoming electronically connected, eventually eliminating auction markets and transaction costs.[6] U.S. securities firms and their clients have been required to accept shortened global standards; for example, settlement eventually will occur in one day following the trade rather than the five-day standard used for decades.

Fixed Commissions. Until 1975, commissions on trades were based on a fixed schedule of fees. Beginning on May 1 of that year, commissions became subject to negotiation, and revenues from some institutional clients declined by more than one-half. Discount brokers quickly entered the business, forcing the wire houses to reduce commissions on retail trades and to develop additional services to attract customers (i.e., the Cash Management Account® offered by Merrill Lynch).

Insider Trading and Other Scandals. Several scandals disgraced prominent securities firms during this period, including:

- The 1970 Goldman Sachs sale of Penn Central commercial paper after the firm had information concerning the railroad's impending bankruptcy
- Insider trading in the late 1980s by various individuals associated with Drexel Burnham Lambert, the most prominent of whom was Michael Milken
- The 1991 Salomon Bros. illegal attempt to corner a U.S. Treasury note sale
- The 1993 Kidder Peabody bond trading fraud committed by one of the firm's employees, Joseph Jett
- The 1994–1995 Baring Brothers $1 billion scandal involving Nick Leeson, an unsupervised trader working in the firm's Singapore branch

THE CURRENT MESS

Until about 1990, stock market analysts operated in relative obscurity and investment bankers worked for financial rewards and the preservation of their integrity and credibility. This situation changed in the 1990s, driven largely by the high-tech and dot-com manias that made quick fortunes for investment bankers despite limited prospects for revenues and profits. Even after stock prices began to decline, several prominent analysts, including Mary Meeker of Morgan Stanley and Henry Blodgett of Merrill Lynch, continued to recommend technology stocks.

Recall our comment in lesson 5 on the ending of restrictions on financial service activities as the result of the passage of the Gramm-Leach-Bliley Act of 1999. This change allowed investment bankers to search for profitable activities throughout financial services. The result has been a refocus on profits and ROE rather than on long-term relationships based on integrity and objective advice. In this environment, some analysts became a part of the sales force rather than independent observers.

Conflicts of Interest

There is growing evidence of a conflict of interest among analysts at the largest brokerage firms, and the SEC has stated that it may institute enforcement cases.[7] Analysts are primarily sales representatives for their employers who participate in road shows to stimulate investor interest and then initiate research coverage. Frequently, analysts were significantly involved in start-up companies before shares were offered to the public, acquiring share ownership at a fraction of the price paid by the public.

Other troubling behaviors include providing advance notice of pending changes in recommendations to their firm's investment bankers. There is even evidence of some analysts acting contrary to their own advice to clients for their own accounts—for example, selling, when advising the public to buy. Compliance departments of securities firms have not been vigilant on analyst conflicts despite numerous instances of troubling behavior.

Securities Firms Respond

The securities industry has been forced to defend itself from congressional oversight, the SEC and other regulators, and angry corporate clients and investors. Public relations statements have been issued declaring the integrity of its employees. For example, in response to various lawsuits against Mary Meeker, Morgan Stanley stated that her "integrity is beyond reproach" and that she "is one of the most respected analysts" in the industry.[8]

More significantly, the Securities Industry Association issued a code of conduct in June 2001 to restore the perception of broker-dealer integrity. By autumn of 2001, 14 Wall Street firms had endorsed the recommendations. The primary intent of the code is to separate the reporting relationships, exchange of unreleased research advice, and basis of compensation of analysts and investment bankers. In addition, some firms have prohibited analysts from ownership of the stocks they cover.

Lawsuits are being filed for a variety of reasons, including investors being duped into IPOs that were overpromoted and corporations being given bad advice. In their biggest years, investment bankers enjoyed revenues approaching $30 billion. As the result, they are a target with "deep pockets," and litigation has been filed contesting several recent investment banking transactions (see Exhibit 9.3).

Threat of Class-Action Suits

The real threat to the securities industry does not come from individual claims but from class-action lawsuits over the handling of IPOs. By 2001, leading class-action attorneys had filed some 500 actions involving over 100 new issues, primarily dot.coms, and more are likely to be filed in the next two years. The eventual cost to the securities firms could be in the billions of dollars.[9]

The most troubling accusation is that underpriced shares were allocated to institutional investors in return for unreasonably high, undisclosed commission charges. A secondary claim, and one that is harder to prove, is the artificial inflation of share prices by the practice of "laddering," or buying stock at increasingly higher prices. When institutions stop buying, prices fall, primarily harming small investors that bought in near the top. SEC rules require disclosure of fees received for advisory or underwriting services, rules that some observers believe can be traced by a forensic accounting review of suspect IPO-related transactions.

EXHIBIT 9.3 Recent Investment Banker Lawsuits

Plaintiff	Defendant[a]	Company	Complaint
Investors	ML, GS, SSB	AT&T Wireless	IPO[b] underwriting negligence
Investors	GS, MS, CSFB, DB, UBS	Turkcell (mobile phones)	IPO underwriting negligence
Investors	CSFB	VA Linux	IPO false and misleading statements
Duke & Co. Customers	Fiserv	Fiserv	Clearing of trades for broker-dealer that committed fraud
Greenville Casino	CSFB	CSFB	Inappropriate financial advice; fee gouging
Log on America	CSFB	Nortel	Inappropriate financial and business advice

[a]Defendants: ML: Merrill Lynch; GS: Goldman Sachs; SSB: Salomon Smith Barney; MS: Morgan Stanley; CSFB: Credit Suisse First Boston; DB: Deutsche Bank; UBS: Union Bank of Switzerland;
[b]IPO = initial public offering
Source: "Suing the Street Over Bum Advice," *BusinessWeek,* March 5, 2001, pp. 102–103.

CONCLUSIONS

The role of the investment banker has changed fundamentally from the provision of thoughtful advisory services and the securing of capital for development and growth, to the hyping of stocks without earnings or prospects. Part of the problem stems from the change in the form of ownership of investment banks from private partnerships to publicly traded companies, which are always focusing on next quarter's earnings announcements.

While there always has been a fiduciary or trust relationship between the industry and its clients, there have been continual problems with scoundrels and unscrupulous individuals. Chief financial officers must be careful in how they use the services of securities firms while protecting the position of existing debtholders and investors.

It is essential to conduct a careful analysis of the integrity and experience of your investment banker. Advice may be professional and objective, or it may be colored to enrich the securities firm. In any event, business reliance on the services of investment bankers must be tempered by the realization that they work primarily for their firms and not for their clients. Ultimately, the securities industry must be subject to the same degree of regulatory oversight as commercial banking, to oversee and prevent unfortunate practices that continue to occur.

NOTES

1. M&A was estimated at about $3.5 trillion in the United States in 2000. For 2001, M&A was down to $1.7 trillion. Data from Thomson Financial, cited in Andrew R. Sorkin, "Merger Business Plunges for Investment Banks. . .," *The New York Times,* January 1, 2002, p. C4.

2. For an interesting account of these ventures, see Niall Ferguson, *The House of Rothschild: The World's Banker,* 1849–1999 (New York: Viking Press, 1999).

3. Quoted at the Pujo hearings on the "money trust" during questioning by committee counsel Samuel Untermyer; "Money Monopoly an Impossibility, Morgan Asserts," *New York Times,* December 20, 1912, pp. 1–3.

4. Calculated from Comptroller of the Currency and Federal Deposit Insurance Corporation data by Anthony Saunders, *Financial Institutions Management,* 3rd ed. (New York: McGraw-Hill, 1999), p. 266, Table 13-3.

5. See the Group of 30 website (*www.group30.org*) and its various publications; i.e., *Clearance and Settlement Systems Status Report* (Washington, DC: The Group of Thirty, Autumn 1992).

6. The Pacific Stock Exchange converted to automated trading in 2000 using the electronic communication network (ECN) Archipelago. For additional information, see Neil Weinberg, "Fear, Greed and Technology," *Forbes*, May 15, 2000, pp. 170–176.

7. Statement by the acting chair, Laura S. Unger, before the House of Representatives Financial Services subcommittee, reported in Gretchen Morgenson, "S.E.C. Leader Cites Conflicts of Analysts At Large Firms," *New York Times*, August 1, 2001, pp. C1–C2.

8. Cited in "Commentary: Wall Street's Chinese Walls Aren't Strong Enough," *Business Week*, August 27, 2001, p. 56.

9. For a discussion of these issues, see Shawn Tully, "Will Wall Street Go Up in Smoke?" *Fortune Magazine*, September 3, 2001, pp. 36–38.

PART 3

Facing Twenty-first Century Challenges

The New Frontier of which I speak is not a set of promises—
it is a set of challenges. It sums up not what I intend to offer the American
people, but what I intend to ask of them.

> John F. Kennedy, speech accepting
> the Democratic presidential nomi-
> nation, July 15, 1960

Audit and Control

What they taught in your MBA finance program:

Auditors provide control and prevent fraud.

What they should have taught:

Auditors are trained as accountants, not as financial managers or as information technology specialists. They do a good job in providing objective reviews of ledgers and journals and in presenting opinions as to the accuracy of the financial statements presented by a company. However, this narrow focus on accounting records causes them to be only vaguely aware of other important control issues: financial control and information control.

WHAT IS CONTROL?

"Control" involves internal and bank (or vendor) actions to monitor operations, identify business risks, and generate relevant data to trigger appropriate responses. These procedures enable managers to run their organizations without fear of the loss of cash or proprietary information and without the establishment of a bureaucracy to monitor behavior. Controls should be developed that are prudent given the limitations in any workplace of cost and the inevitability of human and system errors.

Limits to Control

Control measures are constrained by concerns of economics and concerns of failure.

Concerns of Economics. Control systems could provide nearly absolute reliability if the organization's resources were unlimited. However, any decision on the allocation of corporate resources requires weighing the costs of controls against the benefits from those controls. While there is no simple procedure to calculate the rate of return of control systems, it is clear that some minimal level of investment is necessary to manage business risk.

Concerns of Failure. Many situations involving the failures of established controls have resulted from human or system error in monitoring or implementing the control. For example, a standard cash control is the use of "positive pay." This product allows banks to match the issued and clearing information of checks in controlled disbursement accounts to prevent unauthorized payments.

"Controlled disbursement" is a corporate checking account that provides a total of the checks that will be charged to the accounts each business day by about 10 A.M. EST. The business then has until the close of the day—normally 4 P.M. EST—to fund the account. Failures occur when issued check information is not sent to the bank in a timely manner. The control is circumvented due to the constraints of time, attention, or ignorance, and check fraud can result.

The successful control environment requires a commitment by the CFO to the implementation and operation of control systems. This obligation is expressed in daily interactions with internal staff, customers, and vendors to clearly establish the importance of behavior within an established code of conduct. Responsible behavior as a goal of the enterprise, rather than profits, cost cutting, or shareholder value, is the core philosophy of such companies as Hewlett-Packard, Johnson & Johnson, Walt Disney, and the Marriott Corporation. Their historical focus has been excellence in performance and customer service by establishing principles of conduct and self-improvement.[1]

Problems involving the management of risk or lapses in controls are investigated, corrected, and reviewed for evidence of systemic failures. For example, if an accounts payable mistake occurs, such as the early issuance of a check to a vendor, systems would spot the situation, research would be conducted to determine the reasons, and corrective steps would be initiated. The cause could be innocent, such as miscoded data on a system, or it could be deliberate, such as preferential treatment in violation of policy. In either event, the cause would be isolated and appropriate treatment applied.

Do Auditors Offer Adequate Protection?

We depend on auditors to protect our organizations from risk and control incidents. Traditionally, the accounting profession has provided independent audits of financial records and opinions as to the accuracy of the financial statements presented by the business enterprise. It is not the auditor's job to seek or discover situations involving fraud or to warn the company of possible control failures.

Auditors provide carefully worded opinions regarding the extent of their responsibilities and investigations. Typical language is: "These financial statements are the responsibility of the company's management. Our responsibility is to express an opinion on the statements based on our audits." As audits are currently performed, it is fairly clear that external auditors will not detect a clever fraud. Even when fraud has been detected, auditors have resigned from clients but are under no compulsion to publicly disclose the reasons.

Management looks to auditors for a general review of accounting reports but cannot depend entirely on their ability to protect the organization. Auditors can give an opinion on the fairness of financial data but cannot protect a business against all possible attacks, cannot be at all sites at the same time, and cannot anticipate all possible attacks on an organization's scarce resources.

Control as a Community Responsibility

The search for assistance in establishing secure controls includes the entire community: management and employees, bankers, vendors, customers, and reporting and government agencies. Assume that a payroll check is presented for cashing at a store in a company's locality, and the "employee" has two forms of picture identification. Is this a valid check? There clearly are elements here of community involvement:

■ Your bank, to provide a secure payroll environment
■ The shopkeepers in your town, to ascertain the identity of the "employee"
■ Reporting and government agencies, to oversee and broadcast check fraud activities
■ Your information systems staff, to communicate the fact of a disbursed payroll to the bank and to accounting
■ Your accountants, to make the necessary journal entries and maintain required payroll records

A coordinated effort is clearly required to control fraud, theft, misappropriation, or human or system error.

FINANCIAL CONTROL

Financial control includes actions and products designed to prevent fraud against the corporation. Auditors should not be expected to assist you in selecting products to prevent such dishonest actions as the theft of preprinted check stock, the creation of counterfeit checks using desktop technology, the alteration of legitimate issued checks, and the diversion of funds using electronic payment systems. They will insist on the full reconciliation of outstanding checks and similar actions to find any breaches of your accounting controls, but these approaches tend to be seriously time delayed.

How Fraud Can Occur

Auditors will tell you not to leave piles of cash lying around. They probably told you to be very careful when disbursing large sums of money. But did they tell you that banks have products that can eliminate most employee contact with cash? Did they explain how fraud typically occurs?

Let's examine a case of check fraud. A company issued a check for $50 in payment of a small local purchase. The check was received, stolen, and altered by an employee of the vendor, who used desktop printing technology to make exact copies with the payment amount of $500. The original was then returned for deposit and the clearing of the receivable.

The employee periodically cashed the forged $500 checks, and because they were for relatively small amounts, they escaped notice by the depository bank, the drawee bank, and the company that issued the original $50 check. Sure, the auditors did catch the forgeries, but months had passed, the employee had departed, and the company was out several thousand dollars.

The three most common elements of a financial crime occurred in this situation:

1. A trusted employee was the thief, not some burglar who entered the premises from outside.
2. The fraud involved relatively small sums, because they often fall off your radar screen when reviewing payments or receipts.
3. The crime was facilitated by the fact that the receipts came to an office, allowing access by any employee or passerby, and by the failure of the issuing company to use appropriate bank product safeguards.

How to Prevent This Fraud

The bank products that would have prevented this situation for the payer are *positive* (or *matched*) *pay* and *full account reconciliation*. Full reconciliation involves the matching of issued and paid (or cleared) checks that you have written for payables, payroll, or other disbursements. Reconciliation works with positive pay, which requires that your organization send a file of issued checks each day to your bank. Clearing checks then are matched against a file of issued payments. Any item not matching as to check number and amount is referred to the issuer for rejection or acceptance. Within 10 business days of month-end, you will receive a full reconciliation of your checks.

It is certainly true that auditors look for items that have been altered, counterfeited, or otherwise inappropriately debited (charged) against your bank account. However, they cannot accomplish this in a sufficiently timely manner (i.e., daily) to prevent a determined thief. Furthermore, the all-in cost of an auditor (say $40,000 a year—including salary, benefits, and training) is considerably more expensive than using a bank service (about 10 cents an item for both positive pay and full reconciliation).

PRODUCTS FOR FINANCIAL CONTROL

Do your auditors know about other products that can help with financial controls? Do they audit how these products actually are used?

Lockbox

When checks from your customers are received in your office, you have extended an open invitation for theft by any employee with access to your mail. This is a particular problem if the same individuals have responsibility for cash management and cash application, as may occur in a period of downsizing. In our fraud case, the product that would have prevented the fraud at the receiving company (the vendor) is the lockbox, which places your company's receipts under the control of the bank and out of the hands of your employees.

In a lockbox arrangement, a company informs its customers to send payments to a post office box number in a city with superior mail and check clearing (availability) times. The box is actually maintained by a bank, which retrieves the mail, brings it to the bank's processing center, and deposits the checks received into the company's bank account. The bank provides summary and detailed data on each day's transactions to the company.

Wholesale processing provides check copies and original remittance documents to the client. Retail processing captures encoded scanline information on the bottom of the check and/or remittance documents, which is transmitted to the client in a data file.

Check Printing

Rather than using preprinted check stock, use blank check stock or safety paper. Inexpensive laser technology allows the entire check face, including the MICR (or magnetic ink character recognition) line, to be printed on blank paper. (Special fonts using MICR characters are printed on the bottom of the check to allow automated sorting and processing by the banking system.) Alternatively, you should consider safety or watermark paper, made from multiple layers of colored fibers to cause scarring or bleeding when erased or chemically altered.

Access to Money Transfer Systems

Banks have developed very secure systems to restrict access to money transfer systems, involving password controls; authentication and encryption of messages; and multiple levels of initiation, approval, and release. While you are effectively required to agree to most of these controls at the time of the installation of the money transfer system, many companies loosely monitor actual practice and fail to ensure that employees are following appropriate procedures. For example, passwords are often shared or posted on computer terminals; appropriate money transfer authorizations may be circumvented, such as having different employees set up and release wired payments; and fraudulent phoned instructions for wire transfers are accepted as legitimate.

INTERNAL FINANCIAL CONTROLS

Have your auditors advised you on other essential financial controls?

- *Phony vendors.* Have you verified that your vendors are legitimate businesses and not the associates of an employee in purchasing? Do they all have legitimate tax identification numbers? Has a credit agency conducted a credit check? Do you have their audited financial statements on file?
- *Signature plates.* Do you secure signature plates used in check signing? Have you considered signing your checks electronically?
- *Authorized signers.* How many authorized employees can sign checks? Are former employees still on the authorized signature list maintained by your bank?
- *Multiple check issuance sites.* How many company locations issue checks? Have you considered centralizing all check issuance to improve efficiencies and security?
- *Payroll fraud.* Has your company experienced any payroll fraud? Are your employees issued identification cards, and do such major check cashing locations as supermarkets and financial institutions know how to verify whether they are legitimate? And why are you even issuing payroll checks? Have you considered the direct deposit of your payroll directly into your employees' bank accounts through the ACH (automated clearinghouse)?
- *Theft of bank deposits.* How secure is your process of depositing your office collections? Does your own employee go to the bank, or do you use an armored car service? If an employee carries cash to the bank, have any precautions been taken to protect him or her?
- *Protection of valuable assets.* Have you properly secured areas where valuable company assets are housed? Are locked doors and security alarms installed in sensitive areas?

These concerns should be noted in audit letters or reports. Have your auditors spotted any problems and assisted you with appropriate corrective actions? Your lack of knowledge of any past or current financial control problems in your organization may indicate that they simply haven't been spotted. Nearly every company has had some concerns about its financial controls; it's the wise CFO who detects vulnerabilities and adopts corrective procedures.

INFORMATION CONTROL

As with financial controls, inadequate attention is typically given to safeguarding a most critical corporate asset—information. This failure is due to the widespread responsibilities for information and systems throughout most companies. Auditors, information or computer specialists, operations managers, security personnel—there are many and yet no one is accountable—and all are assumed to have this assignment. For this reason, the CFO should consider assuming responsibility for information control.

The loss of proprietary information through carelessness, theft, or corporate espionage costs tens of billions of dollars each year, with intrusions by and into U.S. and international organizations. Although data are sketchy, only about 5 to 10 percent of all intrusions are detected (according to the Federal Bureau of Investigation), and an even smaller percentage are ever solved and prosecuted. To combat this threat, some $6 billion is spent each year on computer and communications security measures. However, about one-quarter of all U.S. companies have no procedures to safeguard proprietary intelligence.

Value of Information

The resource of value in the twenty-first century new economy organization will be information more than any physical asset, and it is essential to formalize the responsibility for protecting this asset. In order to create the necessary defenses, the CFO should develop a comprehensive plan to identify organizational information vulnerabilities and to develop specific strategies to combat those risks.

Information can have value to the organization in various ways:

- Proprietary knowledge, involving secret marketing, production, personnel, and financial data
- Computer software and hardware, including programs, computers, input/output devices, storage media, telephone lines, and other components of a computer system
- Hardcopy documents, both draft and final, including plans, status reports, manufacturing specifications, working papers, internal correspondence, minutes of meetings, and similar files and papers

Internal Threats to Workplace Information

The integrity of information may be compromised by various internal deficiencies.

Failure to Document Systems.   Although systems engineers and programmers are supposed to flowchart and describe the systems they design, it is unusual to find intact, comprehensive documentation including changes and fixes to the original programs. This is a particular problem when a bank or vendor has participated in the systems installation and then departed, leaving you with the technology but no in-depth explanation of the workings.

Employees.   Employees represent a significant threat to information. They are inside of the organization, know the layout and security measures utilized in most areas of your premises, can be difficult to detect in any wrongdoing, and may perceive that a negative job review, company downsizing, or other adverse job action is legitimate grounds for sabotage or theft.

Employees may take hostile actions for a variety of reasons, including revenge for injustices against themselves or their colleagues, monetary gain, the "challenge," or simply boredom.

Despite the popular media's portrayal of professional criminals as the enemy, the real threat is often the trusted employee.

Vendors and Customers. Organizations tend to establish special relationships with their vendors and certain important customers, allowing casual entry to sensitive areas of a company. While the requirement for visitor badges is common, individuals who frequent your premises may be taken for granted and not observed with the same care as strangers.

During periods when meetings or other contact activities are suspended, vendors and customers routinely have access to telephones, rest rooms, and food vending, which may permit them to observe and eavesdrop on information and computer systems. On company visits we frequently challenge client security and often are allowed to pass security barriers, eavesdrop, or talk our way into protected areas.

Criminals and Competitors

Corporate espionage attempts to compromise security measures while eluding detection in the search for information with potential value. Espionage may involve professionals who steal information for clients, often your competitors, through breaking ("hacking") into your systems. Espionage may take the form of masquerading or social engineering.

- "Masquerading" is the impersonation of a legitimate employee to gain access to a secure area.
- "Social engineering" is a more circuitous approach, involving subterfuges to manipulate employees into revealing confidential information.

Attacks on systems and communications are intended to steal, alter, or disrupt information or to destroy data and computer systems. There are numerous ways to attack your systems and communications, and most of these methods are difficult to detect and prevent.

Trapdoors.   The trapdoor is a back way into a computer program, written by programmers to quickly enter software to update or modify program instructions. Trapdoors often are based on a keyword recognized by the program and known "only" to the programmer. If the intruder can discover the trap door, he or she can gain entry to the computer and probably can access your entire system.

Session Hijacking.   A legitimate system user may leave a workstation temporarily to gather files, use the rest room, attend a meeting, or for other activities. While procedures normally require users to log off, they may fail to do so, expecting to return to their computer shortly or not wanting to be bothered with logging off and logging back on. During this period, any individual could read and/or change files, copy information, or commit acts of sabotage.

Viruses and Trojan Horses.   A virus involves lines of computer code that are inserted into legitimate computer programs to modify and possibly destroy data and software. The virus may replicate itself so that it spreads through a computer system. If data are sent to other computers through the Internet or by copying a file, other computers can become infected. A Trojan horse involves the planting of unauthorized computer instructions inside of a legitimate function, such as commands to enable fraudulent transactions.

Wiretapping and Eavesdropping.   These communications intrusions involve illegal listening on voice or data transmissions. A wiretap uses an electrical tap or connection, usually attached to a junction box, to listen to communications. Eavesdropping uses wireless electronic listening devices for the same purpose.

Falsification of Data.   Data may be altered or falsified at the time it is first recorded. Data such as payroll, sales results, or manufacturing or sales costs also may be changed as it is entered into a computer system. Any alterations that occur during keying or data entry are information or computer systems concerns, and require programs to monitor such activity.

PHYSICAL AND ELECTRONIC PROTECTIONS

Auditors may suggest various "traditional" barriers to entry, including security personnel and guard dogs, and surveillance devices such as cameras and television monitors. These forms of protection assume that an attack will be physical and *overt*. However, current breaches of physical security are usually *covert*, comprising such activities as searching through discarded trash and the interruption of your facilities by utility disruptions and other vandalism.

Employees

The principal defense against people hazards is to hire responsible, trustworthy employees. It is common practice to conduct new-hire reviews with detail appropriate to the responsibility of the position being filled and the commensurate access to company data. Clerical workers who may be hired with minimal background checks often have access to most information systems and can cause extensive damage in that role.

Workers who are hired are seldom subject to subsequent monitoring or review other than for job performance and promotion. Unfortunately, financial problems, family strain, addictions or other psychological illnesses, or other stresses may lead to undesirable behaviors. Organizations should develop monitoring routines, from simple observation or more formalized programs, such as periodic medical examinations and mandatory personal financial statements.

Observation should focus on conspicuous spending, an unusual number of incoming telephone calls, extensive absences from the workplace, changes in physical appearance, and deterioration in job performance. Electronic surveillance or monitoring procedures now exist to eavesdrop on telephone calls and such computer activity as keystroke production and e-mail messages. The law is still developing on employer/employee rights to privacy and notice, and there is a diversity of court rulings on whether employees can be subject to such scrutiny.

Traditional Deterrents

The standard deterrent to physical and people hazards is to establish a locked parameter, allowing access on a need-to-know basis and refusing entry to those not meeting a threshold test. However, companies disclose entirely too much sensitive data through articles, speeches, marketing brochures, websites, government filings, and correspondence, and a competitor often does not have to go undercover to obtain information. To protect corporate secrets, such as strategies and plans, new products and technological innovations, the CFO should designate them as "confidential," restricting distribution.

ELECTRONIC DEVICES AND BARRIERS

Organizations no longer find that locks, alarms, and guard dogs protect their most valuable assets. Current technology and the proliferation of information and systems make it difficult merely to enclose a facility to adequately safeguard technology. Information is on nearly every desk, in every file, and on laptops and other computing devices. Therefore, security begins with prohibiting entry to these areas using electronic devices and barriers.

Entry to computer systems should require positive identification of the individual, using a password, a special key or badge, or an eye or fingerprint scan. Surrounding this secure area should be various types of physical barriers to obstruct intruders, including locked doors and windows, guards and watchdogs, alarmed entries and exits, and surveillance cameras. The barriers should be tested periodically using personnel from outside the area to determine if established procedures are being followed.

Communications Protections

Because of the complexity of communications networks, any exchange of information between computers potentially involves multiple telecommunications connections. The resulting vulnerability from these possible points of intrusion may not be obvious to the computer user but has resulted in countless incidents of eavesdropping, hacking, and theft.

Communications must pass through a firewall barrier to protect internal communications from outsiders (or portions of internal systems from other internal networks). All traffic is reviewed and entry is refused to any message not meeting predetermined criteria. However, in mid-1999 three computer system providers reported that Internet firewall protections were compromised and were invisible to standard antivirus programs.

Telecommunications cables can be wiretapped at nearly any point, inside or outside of your premises, allowing the display and recording of any information being exchanged. Taps can be placed at panels, in walls, at junction boxes, and in tubing placed in dropped ceilings and raised floors prepared for electronic equipment installations. Such cables should be encased in steel or pressure-sensitive conduits; the latter safeguard signals when there has been an intrusion on the line.

Computer Backup Procedures

The regular backing up of computer files was standard procedure when systems were based on mainframe systems and personnel were assigned the task of creating a replacement copy on magnetic tape or other media. Backup procedures typically included retaining logs of backup responsibilities and the off-site storage of such files.

The dissemination of computer systems throughout the modern organization has substantially reduced the CFO's ability to control the timing and procedures for the backing up of files. Many companies deal with this difficult problem by issuing policies (e.g., you *will* back up every night) and hoping that computer users obey. Unfortunately, there have been numerous instances where PCs crash or laptops are stolen, and data are irretrievably lost or the cost and time to re-create them are exorbitant.

The CFO should establish an ongoing audit function to monitor backup procedures on an unannounced basis. A control officer should construct an appropriate backup plan for each program and system, including timing, media, and procedures for file reconstruction. The storage of backup files and records at an auxiliary site should be established in the event of a system crash or other disaster.

Protection of Other Documents

Important information also may exist in noncomputer form. These include evidence of the organization's structure (e.g., incorporation papers, board of directors minutes, lists of stockholders, copies of tax returns, titles to real estate); documents relating to customers, vendors, and employees (e.g., contracts, correspondence, orders, invoices sent/received, payroll data); and documents relating to the protection of intellectual property (e.g., copyrights and patents, licenses, engineering drawings, key employee contracts).

Unfortunately, often these documents are safeguarded somewhat haphazardly, with papers in desks and filing cabinets, vaults, safe deposit boxes, permanent off-site storage, and elsewhere. All important documents should be cataloged and copied onto microfilm or fiche, and a conscious decision should be made as to appropriate storage location and custodian.

Electronic Detection and Surveillance

Programs to detect intrusion to these systems by sounding alerts or displaying warning messages can protect computer and telecommunications systems. Such "alarms" generally identify viruses, unauthorized passwords, repeated password attempts, attempts at entering systems for which the user is not unauthorized, log-ons at an unusual time of day or weekends, and significant changes in usage patterns.

In addition to scanning programs that look for known viruses and programming code patterns, software can monitor patterns in computer processing to detect viruses. These patterns include slowdowns in processing time, programs attempting to write to write-protected media, decreases in computer memory, files that cannot be located, unusual monitor messages, and differences in lengths between active and archival files.

CONCLUSIONS

Accountants and auditors often do an inadequate job in developing finance and information controls. While their review of ledgers and journals certainly is important, many critical activities escape their close examination. The CFO has to get involved in the establishment of financial and information controls. Financial actions include: developing policies and procedures governing financial transactions; carefully reviewing such primary documents as bank statements and account analyses and wire transfer requests; and establishing appropriate controls for such activities as check signing and the office receipt of currency, checks, and securities.

It is equally important to establish adequate controls to secure information. As current practice assigns this responsibility to nearly any (or to no) member of the corporation, it should be considered for the CFO's set of accountabilities. Actions include: documenting current systems; conducting ongoing reviews of employees, particularly those with access to your information systems; constructing adequate physical and electronic barriers; and establishing backup procedures for computer and paper documents and files.

NOTE

1. See James C. Collins and Jerry I. Porras, *Built to Last* (New York: Harper-Business, 1994), particularly chapters 3 and 6.

Risk Management

What they taught in your MBA finance program:

Risk management involves individual functions of insurance,
financial engineering, and safety programs.

What they should have taught:

Many types of risks are embedded in a business operation, going
far beyond the traditional boundaries of finance. The CFO is the
logical manager to develop a comprehensive enterprise risk
management program to identify and quantify these risks and to
develop appropriate programs for their management.

WHAT IS RISK?

Risk is the possibility of loss or injury. Historically, the measurement of risk has been the incidence of human or property
loss in specific categories, such as death or disability by age,
sex, and occupation, or the frequency of fire or weather damage to specific types of construction at various locations. Other
types of risk have been generally recognized but, until recently,
were not managed as a formal management function.

The traditional management of risk has been through insurance, whereby the policyholder accepts a small certain
loss—the premium expense—rather than the possibility of a
large catastrophic loss. Of course, an individual cannot be
"made whole" in a situation involving premature death or a

disabling injury, but the insured or his or her heirs receive money damages as compensation.

Business Risks

Managers often fail to appreciate the extent of risk in normal business operations, due to the fact that much risk is inherent in any transaction. Business risk exists because management's use of the scarce factors of production, land, labor, and capital may result in a lesser return than would have been received if those factors were otherwise employed. The only rational way to deal with such risk is to analyze alternative courses of action continually and to select that action with the greatest return for an acceptable level of risk. If the risk-return relationship from a particular strategy changes, management must adjust its decision accordingly.

Some companies attempt to manage risk by using strategies that avoid the risk. Risk seemingly can be averted by refusing to do business in a particular country, market, or currency. However, by so refusing, you actually are accepting other kinds of risk. As an example, we frequently encounter clients who choose to avoid currency risk by insisting on payment in U.S. dollars. These companies mistakenly assume that they have eliminated risk by this strategy. Instead, they have substituted market risk for currency risk.

In one situation, a Canadian transaction was quoted at U.S. $260,000, or at CD $400,000. An insistence on payment in U.S. dollars would cost the buyer about $10,000, in that the conversion of the Canadian dollar amount to U.S. dollars would yield a price of about $250,000 (with the CD$ at 62 cents as of early 2002). The rational economic decision is to pay in Canadian dollars and hedge by purchasing forward foreign exchange (FX).

The savings in FX are derived primarily from the desire of the Canadian firm to receive the currency of its country for reasons of both convenience and certainty. This situation is often observed when the counterparty is a firm without extensive cross-border experience and limited access to financial markets. A quantitative analysis shows the alternative outcomes. At times when the U.S. dollar must be the transaction currency due to corporate mandate, the transaction may not occur and hence no benefit or loss can be calculated. As the result, the FX transaction risk is hidden by the insistence on U.S. pricing.

UNIVERSALITY OF RISK

Risk often is overlooked because it is everywhere. In lesson 10 we reviewed:

- treasury operation of fraud risk—at the risk of theft, misuse, or loss of funds
- information risk—the risk of the loss of data critical to the operation of your business

We noted earlier that insurance coverage is used to manage risk to life, limb, and property. Other selected categories of business risk are defined in the sections that follow.

Risk Managed Internally

Most business risks are internal to companies and often are managed by the CFO with the assistance of services or external agencies that provide expertise on specific risk issues.

Operational Risk.   *Operational risk* is inherent in business activities, arising from problems with technology, employees, or operations. Often these risks are managed by the establishment of policies and procedures (P&P) to govern the conduct of ongoing activities. Realistically, behaviors cannot be regulated by proclamation. However, assigning specific duties states the company's position on responsibilities, sets a charter for responsible corporate behavior, and assesses penalties should violations occur. See Appendix 11A for additional material and an example of a P&P.

Credit Risk.   *Credit risk* concerns the failure of customers to pay amounts owed and due. We manage these types of risk through credit reports and debt management services provided by such companies as Equifax, Dun & Bradstreet, Trans Union Credit, and TRW Information Services.[1]

Derivative Risk. *Derivative risk* is the concern that the misuse of financial instruments will result in large losses due to adverse moves in interest or currency exchange rates. We monitor derivative risk through the disclosure rules issued by the Securities and Exchange Commission (SFAS 119) and by the Financial Accounting Standards Board (FAS 133).

Companies are required to make quantitative and qualitative disclosures for each category of risk, including interest rate risk, foreign exchange, commodity prices, and other potential market changes of a material nature. A popular evaluation technique is value-at-risk (VaR), which involves a probabilistic assessment of the risk of loss in earnings or cash flows. See the discussion under "Risk Management" in this lesson. Although this lesson does not address derivative risk, numerous published sources are available.[2]

Liquidity Risk. *Liquidity risk* is a company's inability to pay obligations as they come due, resulting in financial embarrassment, a negative impact on the company's credit rating and vendor relations, and potential bankruptcy. This risk is managed by arranging for lines of credit and access to other safety financing.

Foreign Exchange/Interest Rate/Commodity Risk. *Foreign exchange/ interest rate/commodity risk* involve adverse movements in the price of raw materials or financial instruments, causing higher-than-planned costs and possible losses. These risks are hedged by using financial risk management products, including futures, options, swaps, and other instruments.

Risks Managed Externally

Some business risks are managed primarily by external organizations, including rating agencies, various regulators, and other participants in risk oversight. Three types of business risks include:

1. *Financial institution risk,* the possibility that a bank handling your transactions will fail. We monitor bank safety through such organizations as Standard & Poor's, Lace Financial, and Fitch; see lesson 8.
2. *Economic system risk,* the potential for the collapse of the payment system, possibly triggered by some cataclysmic event, which in turn would cause the freezing or loss of assets held in a bank or other depository. This risk is monitored by various U.S. agencies such as the Comptroller of the Currency and the Federal Reserve System and by their counterparts in the various sovereign countries.
3. *Sovereign (or country) risk,* the possibility that a foreign government will interfere with normal business transactions between counterparties due to an economic or political crisis. Recent examples of such actions include the debt moratoria declared by the Brazilian and Mexican governments in the early 1980s and the financial problems of various Asian countries in the late 1990s. We monitor the country stability through evaluation models published by *Euromoney Magazine* and *Institutional Investor.*

RISK MANAGEMENT

The traditional management of these various risks has been through separate programs, the responsibilities for which reside with the CFO and other organizational units. A more comprehensive approach—enterprise risk management (ERM)—is now advocated for the coordinated and integrated administration of risk.

Separate Risk Functions

Risk is managed by surveillance and by policy. Surveillance requires the identification of risk exposures; the development of potential loss estimates, often based on statistics developed to model the occurrence of risk incidents; and contingency planning. Policy involves the establishment of specific procedures for responding to each risk exposure.

Internal specialists have attacked risks for years, but as separate functions.

- Hedgers and credit managers have addressed financial and market risks.
- Lawyers and compliance officers treat regulatory and political risks.
- Insurance buyers acquire coverage for various types of life and health and property and casualty risks.
- Security specialists, occupational safety and health advisors, environmental engineers, and contingency and crisis management planners all work individually toward a safe and secure work environment.
- Financial staff manages derivative, liquidity, foreign exchange, interest rate, and financial institution risks.
- Credit and collection or accounts receivable monitors credit risk.
- Purchasing administers commodity risks.

Comprehensive Enterprise Risk Management

Enterprise risk management identifies, prioritizes, and quantifies the risks from all sources that threaten the strategic objectives of the corporation, including those not previously understood or comprehensively managed.[3] The ERM approach views risk as pervasive in a business and assumes that a coordinated approach through a formal organizational function is necessary to apply twenty-first-century management techniques.

In the absence of ERM, the interdependencies and interrelationships of business risks can be overlooked, resulting in potentially inadequate safeguards for the assets of the enterprise. ERM reduces the volatility inherent in business activities and helps to achieve consistent earnings and manage costs. When calibrated to market conditions, risk management can help a firm determine its true rate of return on investment on a risk-adjusted basis.

The review of financial statements and numerical values (i.e., ratios and costs) ignores many of the risks a company encounters as it does business. Adverse incidents have occurred in various industries, such as the Ford/Bridgestone-Firestone tire recall crisis and the trading losses of Barings Bank that eventually forced it to close. This was recognized in the United Kingdom, where the 1999 Turnbull Report issued by the Institute of Chartered Accountants requires companies listed on the London Stock Exchange to develop a comprehensive risk management program, subject to board of directors' oversight. Risks should be broadly considered in a system of internal controls[4] and not confined to insurance or hedging.

For example, an accepted management approach to purchasing is just-in-time inventory management that we discussed in lesson 2. However, if a disaster, such as a bankruptcy or a fire, affects a vendor, your business activities may be adversely affected. Any usual business activity has risks, which could affect a company's survival in the face of customer dissatisfaction, legal action, Internet disruption (i.e., hacker interference), financing problems, or other incidents.

ENTERPRISE RISK MANAGEMENT PROCESS

The initial ERM involves three separate steps that should be supported by a continuous monitoring process led by the CFO to maintain the comprehensive risk management process[5]:

1. Identifying risk
2. Measuring and prioritizing risk
3. Managing individual and portfolio risk

Identifying Risk

The initial step in ERM is to scan or recognize the elements of a company's business risk. Although various types of risk were noted earlier in the lesson, every organization faces a unique set of risks that must be specified and enumerated. One approach is to assemble a manager focus group or joint application design (JAD), a workshop approach to structured group discussion, to allow the interactive development of risk factors.

Measuring and Prioritizing Risk

Not all risks should be managed proactively, and managers should prioritize and act on those with potential significance to the security of the business. High-priority risks could include the following:

- A marketing decision that could destroy a product or a customer relationship
- Failure to develop technology to meet or surpass the actions of competitors
- Substantial problems with critical information systems (see lesson 10)
- The loss of key management
- Adverse economic conditions that cause increases in the general level of interest rates and the cost of borrowed funds
- Significant regulatory actions by federal and/or state agencies
- Substantial increases in cost factors
- Other actions that would have a serious impact on the accomplishment of the business plan and the survival of the organization

Medium-priority risks would include any actions that could impact the goals in the business plan but do not threaten the company. Examples could include problems with noncritical information systems, difficulties in placing bank credit facilities, and the loss of an intermediate-level manager.

Managing Individual and Portfolio Risk

As we have noted, techniques exist to manage some risks, such as the hedging of selected cost elements, insurance to replace key managers, and the use of financial derivatives to manage interest rate risk. The company must determine the likely occurrence of each risk not yet subject to standard product applications, calculate outcome probabilities, determine the covariance of risk dependencies, and develop appropriate actions. Doing this may involve various organizational factors, including behaviors, capabilities, and culture.

In the future, financial intermediaries will be able to dissect nearly any investment or asset representing a business risk into its most basic components, to create a security that can be marketed to investors. By selling off these asset pieces, the risk of ownership is shifted to investors, who are willing to accept the possibility of a price decline in return for substantial price appreciation. Earlier in the book we used the example of securitizing mortgage loans, which are packaged and sold as securities by banks and other lenders. As investors and users of capital find markets for their needs, the process of financing the business becomes more efficient and the cost of capital falls.

Portfolio hedging involves recognizing the interdependence of risk factors which move in consistent or in conflicting relationships. ERM techniques that will emerge will involve multifunctional "hybrid" products, including insurance, capital markets, financial derivatives, and other product areas. Since risks vary by industry and even by company, ERM will build on basic solutions to meet the requirements of each organization.

Value-at-Risk

Value-at-risk is one approach to determining the risk exposure in a portfolio of assets.[6] Although certain risks (e.g., financial instruments, credit, commodity prices) can be forced into the VaR model, VaR is an expensive process that is heavily dependent on historical patterns. Other risks are not subject to the same statistical calculations and may be inadequately considered. Some companies using VaR supplement their analysis by stress testing to determine likely performance in various worst-case scenarios.

Value-at-risk calculates the amount of risk inherent in a financial portfolio with a predefined confidence level (usually 95 percent), including risk covariance. Various proprietary products model this risk situation, with the most respected possibly being CreditMetrics developed by J.P. Morgan Chase. A major advantage of VaR is the highlighting of lines of business requiring substantial investment or incurring high risk levels yet producing low profits.

The major disadvantage—other than the significant cost—is the inherent dependence on historical trends, which may fail as a guide to specific future events. This was precisely the situation encountered by Long-Term Capital Management (LTCM) when capital markets suddenly became illiquid and yield spreads (the difference in interest rates between two or more securities) between U.S. Treasury securities and noninvestment-grade debt (commonly referred to as "junk" bonds) increased beyond historical relationships.

Investors panicked during recent Russian and Asian political and economic crises, and the situation was exacerbated by thin trading (and illiquid global markets) in August 1998. The losses of highly leveraged hedge funds (funds that invest directly in securities and through derivative instruments to increase their leverage) were amplified, as positions had to be liquidated to meet margin calls. LTCM made matters worse by using derivatives to increase its investment position.

Computer model simulations typically do not anticipate the "perfect storm" (or worst-case) scenario, when all factors are adverse at the same time. This phenomenon is sometimes known as model risk, resulting from bad pricing data or an inadequate modeling structure. The latter can occur when markets are illiquid, which often occurs in obscure markets (i.e., emerging economies). Since a historical pattern can be misleading in a specific circumstance, VaR can be tested to determine the performance of a portfolio in a worst-case situation.

CONCLUSIONS

Your graduate finance program taught that risks are managed using various financial products, including insurance, options, futures, swaps, and other derivative instruments. However, there are many other risks inherent in operating a business, and the CFO needs to recognize, measure, and manage these risks in a comprehensive ERM program. In addition, ERM can assist in determining a company's risk-adjusted rate of return on its capital investments when measured against market conditions.

NOTES

1. See David Schmidt, "Credit & Collections: Charlatans at the Gate," *Controller Magazine,* September 1997, pp. 49–53.

2. See, e.g., Robert J. Schwartz, ed., *Derivatives Handbook: Risk Management and Control* (New York: John Wiley & Sons, 1997); or Carol Alexander, ed., *Risk Management and Analysis: Measuring and Modelling Financial Risk* (New York: John Wiley & Sons, 1999).

3. See James Deloach and Nick Temple, *Enterprise-Wide Risk Management: Strategies for Linking Risk & Opportunity* (Paramus, NJ: Financial Times Prentice Hall, 2000).

4. See *Internal Control,* Guidance for Directors on the Combined Code, §20, and Appendix, §1, which cites such risks as market, credit, liquidity, technological, legal, health, safety, environmental, reputation and business probity. This document is available at *www.icaew.co.uk/internalcontrol.*

5. This approach is based on Robert Schneier and Jerry Miccolis, "Enterprise Risk Management," *Strategy and Leadership,* March/April 1998, pp. 10–14.

6. Recent discussions include Cormac Butler, *Mastering Value at Risk: A Step-By-Step Guide to Understanding and Applying VaR,* (Englewood Cliffs, NJ: Financial Times Prentice-Hall, 1999); Kevin Dowd, *Beyond Value at Risk: The New Science of Risk Management* (New York: John Wiley & Sons, 1998); and Philip W. Best, *Implementing Value at Risk* (New York: John Wiley & Sons, 1999).

Guide to the Preparation of Policies and Procedures

A policy and procedure (P&P) begins with a statement of *applicability* (to which business units does the policy pertain?) and *purpose* (what are the two or three goals of the policy?). Next, provide a *statement* of the P&P, and the specific corporate action expected. Then write *guidelines* covering definitions of terms used, specific limits on actions, forms and systems to be used, and other procedural issues. A complete *sequencing of required actions* should be provided, indicating all essential steps in the action being discussed. The following P&P illustrates this process.

INFORMATION MANAGEMENT

Purpose

The purpose of this policy is to state the position of the COMPANY on the protection of the data and information systems used by the COMPANY in the conduct of its activities. Information has significant value and requires as high a level of protection as would be accorded a physical asset, cash, or an employee of the COMPANY. Measures shall be developed to safeguard data and information systems against damage, alteration, loss, or unauthorized disclosure.

Policy

Data and the information systems that generate that data are valuable assets of the COMPANY, and shall be protected by all reasonable efforts from inappropriate disclosure, loss, damage, or destruction. Designated System Owners have specified responsibilities for information, as discussed in this policy. However, all employees are accountable to protect these resources and will be held answerable for their actions should data or information systems be compromised by their deliberate or careless actions.

This policy applies to all information in development or owned by the COMPANY, whether as paper, electronic, or other media, and to all systems used to create, manage, or store that information, including mainframe and personal computers, and communication devices.

Procedures

System Ownership. Information and systems may be acquired through a procurement process or developed internally. Once corporate control is established, a specific manager will be designated as the owner of the information system (the "System Owner") to ensure that adequate protection is provided. All information resources (hardware, software, facilities, data, and telecommunications) will be assigned to an owner (defined as a functional position). For example, the "owner" of the resources contained within a general support system may be the manager of that facility. Resources located within user areas (i.e., offices or laboratories) may be "owned" by the manager of those areas.

To assist with the determination of ownership, individual system boundaries must be established. A system is identified by logical boundaries being drawn around the various processing, communications, storage, and related resources. These assets must be under the same direct management control with essentially the same function, reside in the same environment, and have the same characteristics and security needs. System Owners—

those managers most directly affected by and interested in the information or processing capabilities—must demonstrate how they are planning to protect information and processing capabilities from loss, misuse, unauthorized access, modification, unavailability, or undetected security-related activities.

The Security Administrator will define the scope and format for security plans to ensure a standardized approach that provides sufficient information to assess the security posture. Factors to be considered in the determination of ownership are: the originator or creator of data; the organization or individual with the greatest functional interest; and physical possession of the resource.

The responsibilities of the System Owner include the following:

- Acceptance of and conformity to governing confidentiality and licensing or use agreements as established by information system vendors
- Determination that employees and other users are trained in the operation of the system
- Insistence that system users have appropriate permission and password access
- Evaluation of the appropriate level of security required for the protection of the system
- Assurance that adequate information documentation and system/file backup is established and maintained

Documentation and System File Backup.   Data and information systems are valuable assets and must be protected by the creation of systems documentation and backup files. The backing up of information system files involves the creation of duplicate copies at appropriate intervals consistent with the sensitivity and value of the data. This backing up will enable the efficient restoration of systems in the event of a crash or the deliberate or accidental damage/destruction of data or files.

Backup copies of information systems are to be maintained at a secure site to replace damaged or destroyed originals. The determination of the frequency of backups shall be based on the value of the information to the organization and the viability of alternative approaches to reconstructing any lost data, such as reentering input records. Because of the variation in the criticality of information, the System Owner, working in cooperation with the Security Administrator, will determine the frequency and format of the backup. Logs of backups will be maintained, indicating the time, date, and operator conducting the backup.

Documentation is used to establish the sequence of actions in an information system including descriptions of the hardware and software, policies, standards, procedures, and information system security measures. While most documentation is in the form of flowcharts that depict information system elements in a logical flow, any of the following formats is acceptable:

- Vendor-supplied documentation of hardware/software
- Application requirements
- Application security plan
- General support system(s) security plan(s)
- Application program documentation and specifications
- Testing procedures and results
- Standard operating procedures
- User manuals

Such documentation makes possible the maintenance and revision of changes to information systems.

Critical/Major Applications.   All applications require some level of security, and adequate security for most of them should be provided by security of the general support systems in which they operate. However, certain applications, because of the nature of the information they contain, require special management oversight and should be treated as critical or major, as designated by senior management.

A major or critical application is any use of information systems or networks that would seriously impact the ability of the organization to perform its mission if that application were altered or unavailable. Examples of critical applications are personnel systems, billing systems, financial or billing systems, and the like. Since most users spend the majority of their information system time interacting with one of these major applications, particular emphasis on security awareness and education should be integrated into the training and documentation for these systems.

Self-Assessment.   To ensure adherence to this policy, the COMPANY will conduct a self-assessment review every six months. The review will be conducted by teams comprised of the Security Administrator and System Owners. The primary purpose of the self-assessment is to determine adherence to the requirements outlined in this policy.

Required Actions

The COMPANY will designate a System Owner at the time of the acquisition or completed development of an information system. The manager so designated will be a principal user of the resource, with adequate knowledge and training to protect its integrity. The System Owner, with the counsel of the Security Administrator, will develop specific procedures to accomplish the tasks listed in this policy and accompanying procedures.

It is essential that the System Owner actively participate in the development of appropriate security measures, including the training of employees and documentation and system/file backup. Self-assessments are intended to provide constructive feedback for specified deficiencies. However, continued System Owner deficiencies may result in appropriate disciplinary actions.

The Chief Financial Officer's Focus

What they taught in your MBA finance program:

CFOs have financial responsibilities for the company, principally minimizing capital costs and maximizing returns.

What they should have taught:

CFOs are effectively "co-executives" with the CEO or chairman. Along with the senior managers for information, marketing, and manufacturing, their responsibility is to lead the company through the extremely complex and dynamic business and economic conditions of the twenty-first century.

THE CHIEF FINANCIAL OFFICER'S EMERGING ROLE

Throughout this book, we have endeavored to demonstrate that the responsibilities of the CFO have changed significantly since you went to school. A major driver for these changes has been the evolution of the business organization to the new economy model, with intellectual capital becoming more important than the traditional classical factors of production: land, labor, and financial capital. As ideas and creativity take precedence over manufacturing and assembly-line workers, the old organizational line-and-staff form of governance becomes irrelevant.

Line-and-staff is a terrific concept if you are managing the Roman legions or the Catholic church. It hasn't been as successful when applied to the modern corporation, where instead of the primary goal being the maximization of shareholder value, it has been a derivative goal of business units acting independently. Coordination and cooperation in the overall business effort suffers, and senior management often does not know what the business units are doing.

Old Chief Financial Officer Model

In one situation, a manufacturing company with long production times and aging inventories attempted to improve margins by integrating the production sites of its separate businesses and by eliminating redundant functions. The CFO had elaborate costing developed to show returns by product line and market and, using cash flow reengineering techniques, developed specific recommendations for internal improvements and outsourcing.

Because the CEO had spent much of his time on external matters, including analysts' meetings and public relations, he did not appreciate the independence of the affected business units. The project failed due to a lack of senior manager cooperation, and eventually the entire production process was moved to a country where costs to manufacture were lower, resulting in the loss of 3,000 U.S. jobs.

New Chief Financial Officer Model

The board of directors of this company eventually lost confidence in the CEO, citing such problems as labor-management distrust, the lack of business unit cooperation, disappointing ROEs, and the loss of key customers. A new CEO was selected from among the more successful of the business groups. He had been exposed to the various functions of the company through visits, training, and peer interaction.

The new CEO focused his efforts on rebuilding the morale of the organization and on improving the company's image to external constituencies. While the heads of marketing, manufacturing, and information all cooperated to accomplish these objectives, the CFO developed alternative plans to achieve the returns expected by investors and lenders. These plans included actions to accomplish the maximum cash flow for the company, supported by a realistic financing strategy.

Chief Financial Officer as "Co-President"

As we have seen, the CFO's role has to broaden to become a sort of co-president with the CEO. Others included in this office-of-the-executive management approach include the senior information officer, the chief marketing officer, and the executive vice president for manufacturing. It is only through the CFO's active participation in operating and strategic decisions that the kinds of mistakes noted in the prologue can be avoided.

The CFO's responsibilities become considerably more than managing the cost of capital, determining that accounting entries are correct, and ascertaining that appropriate insurance coverages are secured. His or her position requires an intimate knowledge of the core elements of the business enterprise regardless of their traditional assignment, while working in concert with other senior managers to optimize operational processes. These actions are required to fulfill the CFO's basic responsibilities to the organization.

In the third millennium the CFO is now playing and will play numerous roles that are quite different from those of the last century. In the sections that follow, we review selected activities in the more formalistic old economy and in the dynamic new economy.

FINANCE'S ORGANIZATIONAL FOCUS

What is the orientation of finance as it functions within the organization? In the old economy, it was providing capital and accounting reports. In the new economy, the role is being significantly expanded into nearly every significant business area.

Old Economy

Finance traditionally has been a staff function separated from other line and staff activities, focused on accounting, treasury, and insurance matters. In many companies, this isolation is overcome only at the senior manager level, usually in cabinet-type meetings involving the various chiefs of departments and the chief executive/operating officer. This phenomenon often is referred to as the "silo" effect, which is essentially the "us" against "them" mentality without regard to the collective needs of the organization.

Direct reports to the CFO typically have not been concerned with the operations of the business and often do not have any idea what debits or credits are referring to in the real-world of inventories, labor, and sales. Comptrollers, treasurers, and other financial managers do not accompany the sales force on customer calls, or spend any significant time on the production line, or investigate information systems issues. Instead, they tend to remain in the friendly confines of their offices, largely clueless as to the meaning of the numbers on their computer screens.

This attitude is tolerated by the boss—the CFO—who isn't really managing finance. Financial management means the development and implementation of integrated strategies for the business enterprise. If any management is being attempted, it's the numbers being reported to ratings agencies, stock analysts, investment bankers, and the board of directors. Unfortunately, the demands for instant information and results that meet or beat forecasts have become the focus of many senior managers.

New Economy

The silo mentality is ending at many companies, largely because of the growing recognition of the interrelationship among all functions in a business. There are various reasons for this attitudinal change, including competition, cost of capital, and transaction finance.

Competition.   Customer and vendor relationships have generally been friendly, based on long-established counterparty relationships. The future business environment will demand a more aggressive response to global competition, with the penalty for apathy the loss of market position, perhaps one that has been secure for decades. The CFO shares responsibility for ensuring that his or her company is productive and efficient, which requires ongoing interaction with other elements of the business.

Cost of Capital.   The significant increase in the cost of debt and equity capital in the last three decades forces CFOs to really understand and participate in decisions regarding the investment of capital in projects with suspect future returns. This development requires financial manager immersion in many of the activities of the business and the accompanying destruction of silo barriers.

Transaction Finance.   Although debits, credits, and financial reporting will always exist, the process of financial decision making in the "old" and "new" economies is not similar. The old economy involves discrete activities, time for thoughtful decision making, and only a cursory concern for discounted cash flow valuations. The new economy involves continuous activities, real-time decisions, and concern for discounted cash flow returns with consideration for the high cost of capital. The new discipline of "transaction finance" addresses these issues.[1]

For additional discussion of finance's role in the twenty-first-century organization, see lesson 3.

BUDGETING AND ACCOUNTING

How are budgeting and accounting activities handled? In the old economy, managers relied on fixed budgets, which quickly became obsolete. In the new economy, dynamic planning is a requirement and the only certainty is change.

Old Economy

Budgeting and accounting often are considered to be necessary financial activities although of limited usefulness in actually managing a business. Accounting debits and credits result in journal entries that enable the accountant to prepare trial balances and financial statements. All of this records the past, both in terms of actual costs and revenues and in their relationships to volumes and profits. Costs often are reported using conventions that distort the actual costs incurred, as with LIFO inventory accounting (which assumes that the last item purchased is the first to be sold).

In international business, companies have been accustomed to the reporting of financial results by country, with local currencies, language, and customs driving accounting decisions. While statements are consolidated for the purpose of global reporting, little management information has been available to determine product, customer, or market profitability.

Budgeting obviously is necessary to control expenditures over the coming fiscal period, usually one year. However, the process is often static, in that once established, budgets are difficult to change to reflect new opportunities and challenges. Revenues assume a continuation of past pricing trends, which may change significantly in inflationary or deflationary times or in the face of predatory competitors. Costs likewise assume past relationships, despite such events as overtime; severe materials shortages related to demand, weather, or other influences; or rising energy costs.

New Economy

As the CFO extends his or her domain beyond the finance silo, he or she will be able to see practical applications of budget and accounting reports that actually assist senior managers in decision making. The interrelationship of business functions will require reliable, nearly real-time information on how each element of the business is performing rather than lifeless budget reports of little relevance to anyone except the affected managers.

International change drivers include competition from the European Union (EU) and the acceptance of the euro as the currency of most of Europe, allowing the development of meaningful global financial statements based on product profitability. The euro (and the British pound if the U.K. chooses not to participate in the euro) will require consistent definitions of accounting data, standardized systems, and a single currency for all transactions.

Planning will be continuous, based on real-time accounting data compiled and available on an ongoing basis. As the result, accounting closings will be virtual, with reports issued within hours rather than 10 to 15 days after the end of the fiscal period. Budgets will be revised based on a continuous stream of data on sales, expenses, profits, competitive actions, and results vs. plan. Profitable activities will be discovered and rewarded; marginal ventures will be reviewed for inefficiencies, and decisions made as to corrective action. This process will include the allocation of capital and arrangements for financing and will save thousands of hours of accounting effort.

MERGERS AND ACQUISITIONS

How are merger and acquisition opportunities evaluated? In the old economy, corporate finance procedures examined discounted cash flow projections based on cost of capital estimates. In the new economy, decisions will be based on global portfolio theory incorporating the measurement of risk and the potential impact on future profits.

Old Economy

For the past half century, corporate finance has utilized discounted cash flow techniques to evaluate investment alternatives, both for internal expansion and for merger and acquisition activity. A capital investment typically is assumed to be accretive by the end of the first year, with positive incremental benefits through a combination of revenue enhancements and cost reductions. However, probably three out of four

M&A deals are disappointments, due to a combination of excess premiums paid; bad advice from investment bankers; morale and leadership problems, particularly in the acquired company; and timing and execution.

Many deals appear to be motivated by the desire to please investor and analyst demands for growth, which inevitably is faster through acquisition than through internal expansion. As the result, many mergers have been between similar types of businesses, resulting in a sort of "buying" of customers rather than the thoughtful construction of a portfolio of assets to manage shareholder risk.

New Economy: Economic Issues

While increases in revenues and the customer base—along with reductions in costs—will continue to be an essential element in M&A decisions, CFOs will emphasize the construction of a portfolio of investments that diversify the risks and returns for the enterprise. Merger problems often arise because of the positive correlation of the returns from each component of the new organization, causing increased ROEs in boom times but losses in recessions.

Conscious decisions to diversify risk by merging complementary businesses can assist in reducing joint risk while improving the possibility of a successful long-term strategy. M&A activity can assist in the restructuring of large old and new economy companies by such asset realignment, to improve shareholder returns and discard underperforming assets.

Furthermore, overemphasis on concentration within an industry may increase the possibility of an antitrust review, regardless of the orientation of the political party in power. Large mergers may injure customers, reduce innovation, cost thousands of jobs, and stifle competition, and do not always lead to greater efficiency and profits. The new M&A megadeals like Citigroup, DaimlerChrysler, and AOL Time Warner have been allowed to proceed so long as competition is maintained. Where it is not, as in the Microsoft case (see lesson 5) or in the

United Air Lines–U.S. Airways merger, opposed by the Justice Department, litigation may result.

New Economy: Accounting Issues

In addition, CFOs will be forced to deal with the write-down of assets whose value has declined from their acquisition cost, regardless of whether the purchase was for cash or stock. This requirement is the result of new Financial Accounting Standards Board rules that force companies to be realistic about the carrying cost of goodwill. The new regulations require a reevaluation at least once a year, and many expect to realign values every quarter.

This action will affect companies that paid premiums for technology as the general level of market valuations fell; in early 2002, the NASDAQ index was down more than one-half from its all-time high in the year 2000. The determination of fair value can be calculated based on the market value of comparable publicly traded companies, but many of these have suffered serious recent price declines.

Business Week calculates that the potential write-down for a group of 12 corporations is $85 billion, with several telecommunications and high-technology companies included in the group.[2] In some instances the write-down exceeds current stockholders' equity, which would effectively destroy all of the equity holders' value. The problems of the telecommunications industry discussed in the Introduction would be compounded by the write-down rule. For example, Nortel, which lost $19.2 billion in the second quarter of 2001, will write-down $12.3 billion for nearly worthless acquisitions.

FINANCIAL DECISION SUPPORT

How are financial decisions made? In the old economy, strategic business unit, division, or product profitability was derived from traditional accounting data. In the new economy, activity-based costing and other activity-focused profitability systems will be utilized to support dynamic decision making, using prices and costs at varying cost of capital assumptions.

Old Economy

A substantial portion of financial information is dependent on accounting protocols that may be inappropriate to new economy requirements. Although we are not permitted to account for people on the balance sheet, they are the most important resource of the new economy.

Industries built on intellectual capital generally have high market price-earnings ratios: pharmaceuticals (38 times), publishing (57 times), image types of consumer products (e.g., personal care and cosmetics, 33 times), and computers (31 times). Repetitive process industries generally have low P/Es, including manufacturing (22 times), public utilities (20 times), and construction (15 times).[3]

The development of useful old economy financial data is also affected by the requirement for conservative accounting treatment, the lumping together of costs that may be incurred for very different activities, and the dilemma of unavoidable costs in developing pro forma analyses. Accounting data were satisfactory for old economy uses but largely irrelevant in managing intellectual capital.

New Economy

Activity-based costing, described in lesson 4, is one useful attempt to overcome these problems and more closely align financial data. However, ABC addresses only the issue of entries recognized by traditional ledger accounting, reconfiguring those expenses by logical business activity or function.

The valuation of intangibles and intellectual property has never been supported by the accounting profession, with the result that companies often ignore the strategic benefit of patents, copyrights, brands, dominant marketing position, special customer relationships, and their own employees. The entire capital allocation decision requires that some measure be assigned to these assets in order to develop an accurate assessment of costs and revenues. The Financial Accounting Standards Board and the Securities and Exchange Commission recently have encouraged supplemental financial reporting to track such intangibles, and it is likely that the accountants eventually will participate in this endeavor.[4]

INFORMATION TECHNOLOGY

What role does the CFO have in information technology (IT)? In the old economy, decisions on IT were made by the senior information officer and supported by the CFO. In the new economy, the CFO is an equal partner with IT.

Old Economy

Information systems—often known as MIS (management information systems) or IT —have been a dominant force in the investment of business capital in recent decades, beginning with mainframe computers, and later with systems enhancements, enterprise resource planning (ERP) systems, telecommunications equipment, and workstation computing. However, the focus of MIS/IT is the viability of technology, not the financial implications of such initiatives.

In fact, senior management often has written a blank check to MIS/IT, partially in awe of computer nerds but also due to fear of losing ground to competitors. Sometimes the investment was well advised; sometimes it was an open sinkhole for money. Regardless, finance seldom interfered, failing to ask reasonable questions regarding forecast cash flows (mostly "out"), IRRs, or the impact of these investments on future ROEs.

New Economy

Despite the collapse of many Internet stocks in the 2000–2001 period, some observers believe that the business-to-business market will grow to the trillions of dollars by the end of this decade. E-commerce allows user-friendly interaction between buyers and sellers of products and services, access to global markets, and minimal transaction costs. Further impetuses are dissatisfaction with the rigid protocols of electronic data interchange, the expense and time required to implement EDI formats, and the continuing desire to convert paper to electronics.

Many CFOs still believe that e-commerce and other technology initiatives are not within their domain and should be the responsibility of MIS/IT. The financial implications of these investments do not permit this attitude of disassociation, and CFOs must work cooperatively with MIS/IT to ensure that the appropriate decisions are made for capital allocated to information systems.[5]

GLOBAL ECONOMY

What role does the CFO have in global economic analysis? In the old economy, the CFO accepted economic conditions and did little or no analysis or interpretation of global geopolitical events. In the new economy, the CFO must be an international economist, concerned both with changing world conditions and the development of appropriate responses.

Old Economy

In the old economy, the CFO was concerned primarily with the economy of the business's domicile and largely ignored international economic concerns. If markets existed in other countries for a company's goods and services, the lure of incremental sales was met by exporting domestic production. In fact, only in recent years has comprehensive marketing research been conducted on global markets—led by such companies as Ford Motor and Coca-Cola—in the search for business or consumer demand that has not yet been saturated.

Economics was a subject for banks and other financial institutions and for the mandatory Business 101 class in your sophomore year of college. Foreign exchange and interest rate differentials were too arcane to understand. Besides, any foreign exchange exposure could be hedged (at least in the major currencies) using futures contracts. The global old economy offered a natural multinational hedge: When the domestic economy was weak, product could usually be sold abroad.

For example, capital spending declined in the United States in the 1986–1987 period but remained strong in Europe. Conversely, capital spending rose sharply in the United States in 1993 but declined in Europe and Japan.[6] CFOs were grateful for the business opportunity, although few attempted to understand or anticipate these events.

New Economy

Europe's historical fragmentation and mistrust has largely ended with the creation of the European Union, the euro, and the European Central Bank. While Germany and France may have fought three great wars in less than a century, they are now in a strategic partnership with 13 other countries—Belgium, Italy, Luxembourg, the Netherlands, Denmark, Ireland, the United Kingdom, Greece, Spain, Portugal, Austria, Finland, and Sweden, with 13 Eastern and Southern European countries considering membership.

While it is unlikely that the euro or the EU will replace the U.S. dollar or economy, the $6 trillion gross domestic product (GDP) of Europe and the $4 trillion GDP of the countries of the Far East will compete with the United States for world markets. As businesses begin to interconnect through e-commerce, capital flows, intellectual capital, and technology, the global economy simultaneously suffers recession or enjoys prosperity.

A further concern is sovereign risk, the interference of commercial operations or debt repayment by foreign governments, causing a shift in investor attitudes in reaction to these geopolitical forces. A sudden devaluation or change of government can cause a serious reaction in the financial markets as investors search for safety and return. Therefore, it is necessary to observe country stability in making decisions about future business opportunities.

The CFO cannot afford to regard cross-border economic activity as a marginal consideration, because there is no longer an economy based on national borders. An important new role for the CFO is to monitor global economic activity, search for shifts in product or service demand that may affect sales, manage manufacturing and marketing costs, and develop contingency plans that can respond to these changes.

CONCLUSIONS

The CFO faces an incredibly complex and dynamic business environment, one in which he or she will be as important to the success of the business as the chairman or CEO. The dozen areas discussed in this book are extremely important and represent ways the CFO must participate in the strategic *and* operational activities of the enterprise. This busy agenda will drive the CFO's roles in the next century.

NOTES

1. See James Sagner, *Financial and Process Metrics for the New Economy* (New York: AMACOM, 2001).
2. "Today, Nortel. Tomorrow. . . ," *Business Week,* July 2, 2001, pp. 32–35, at 33.
3. All P/E ratios are reported as the market price as of July 26, 2001, divided by earnings per share, and stated as "times." "Corporate Scoreboard, Second Quarter 2001," *Business Week,* August 13, 2001, pp. 77–95.
4. See Floyd Norris, "Seeking Ways to Value Intangible Assets," *New York Times,* May 22, 2001, p. C2.
5. One commentator sees the "CFO as E-Business Architect," the title of Marlene Piturro's article in *Strategic Finance,* September 2001, pp. 25–29.
6. See Michael Mandel, "In a One-World Economy, a Slump Sinks All Boats," *Business Week,* June 25, 2001, p. 38.

What Have We Learned about Finance?

Take any corporate finance text and thumb through the pages. Then ask yourself if you are looking at a finance book or a math book. Like most fields in the social sciences, finance attempts to measure relationships that often cannot be logically quantified. In this book, we have spent considerable space debunking such measures, including profits and ROE (lesson 1), measures of working capital (lesson 2), various time value of money (TVM) measures (lessons 5 and 7), and value at risk and other risk management measures (lesson 11).

The idea that inductive relationships exist based on a mathematical calculation is appealing but does not necessarily mean that such an exercise is correct. Given the complexity of large organizations, the number of variables implicit in any decision or course of action makes such simplistic efforts largely futile.

You should instead consider the universality of finance in the twenty-first century business. As we discussed in lesson 3 and again in lesson 12, the CFO's responsibilities traverse every functional area of a business and demand that finance participate in significant operational activities and strategic decision making. Operational concerns focus primarily on the management of costs and working capital (lessons 1, 2, 4, 6, and 10), while strategic concerns include access to the debt and equity markets (lessons 5, 8, and 9), strategic planning (lesson 7), and risk management (lesson 11).

These assignments are very different from the finance presented in your MBA program, because that finance assumed a structure based on an old economy, line-and-staff organization. The new economy of the twenty-first century changes every preconceived notion, forcing total CFO involvement in the management of the business.

SO ... WHAT WAS "RIGHT" ABOUT YOUR MBA PROGRAM?

- Your tuition bill and requests for alumni contributions.
- The idea that learning is a lifelong experience.
- Debits are entries on the left side and credits are entries on the right side.

Not much else!

index

209